DESERT SOUTHERN CALIFORNIA— REVIEW COMMENTS

The silent desert conceals its fabulous past unless you travel with a shelf full of books, a bus-load of old-timers, or this single volume by Choral Pepper.

—Dr. David J. Webber
Past-president of the Western History Association,
Professor of History at Southern Methodist University

Desert Lore of Southern California is a testimonial to an older California, a different California, when matters of life and death were more important than matters of lifestyle.

—James Curran
Reviewer, *The San Bernardino Sun*

Factual yet reads like an adventure novel, an excellent job of combining history, myth, and travel tips.

—Dr. Iris H.W. Engstrand
Professor of History at the University of San Diego,
Board chair of editorial consultants for the *Journal of History*.

An expertly researched and endlessly fascinating narrative of historical vignettes and legends, accompanied by detailed maps of the region.

—Richard W. Crawford
Archivist of the San Diego Historical Society

An entertaining collection...much appreciated by desert enthusiasts, it emphasizes myths, legends, and yarns.

—Dr. Eugene Keith Chamberlin
Historian, Squibob Chapter, E Clampus Vitus

A magical blend of myth, legend, and very real history...wonderful tales, some long out of print and some fresh...this book will remain a permanent and well thumbed addition to your bookcase or backpack.

—Steven Bogdan
Historian, Imperial County Historical Society

CP

Desert Lore of Southern California

Second Edition

Choral Pepper

*One in a series of
Sunbelt Natural History Guides*

SUNBELT PUBLICATIONS
SAN DIEGO

Cover Design by Patton Bros. Design & Graphics
Book design by October Publishing Services
Maps by Lowell Lindsay, Map Graphics by Court Patton
Printed in the United States of America

All inquiries should be directed to Publisher:

Sunbelt Publications, Inc.
P.O. Box 191126
San Diego, CA 92159-1126
(619) 258-4911 (619)258-4916 fax

02 01   5 4 3 2

Library of Congress Cataloging-in-Publication Data
    Pepper, Choral.
    Desert Lore of SouthernCalifornia / written by Choral
      Pepper.— 2nd ed.
        p.   cm. — (Sunbelt Natural History Guides)
    Includes bibliographical references and index.

      ISBN 0-932653-26-X
      Second Edition 1999.
1. Deserts—California, Southern—Guidebooks. 2. Folklore—
California, Southern. 3. Desert ecology—California, Southern—
Guidebooks. 4. California, Southern—History, Local.
5. California, Southern—Guidebooks.   I. Title.   II. Series
F867.P47 1999
979.4'990453—dc21   98-27669
                                                  CIP

Photo Credits are listed in their respective captions with individual contributor codes as follows:
CP – Choral Pepper   DEL – Diana Lindsay
LEL – Lowell Lindsay   JRL – Jon Lindsay

*This book is dedicated to my son Trent
and grandsons Erik and Alex*

CP

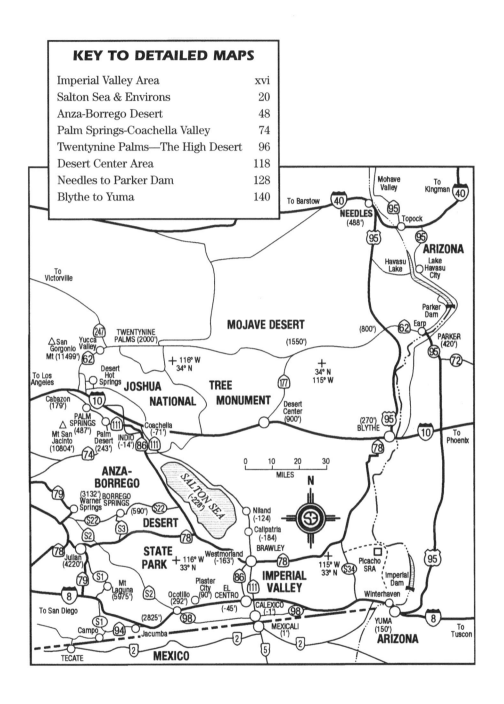

KEY TO DETAILED MAPS

Desert Lore Of Southern California

Second Edition

TABLE OF CONTENTS

FOREWORD

The California desert has always been a magnet for adventurous souls— attracting wayfarers to its beautiful, mysterious and at times inhospitable or even deadly reaches with rumors of brilliant gold, fabled treasure, hidden wisdom, or the chance to renew life. If you have ever heard the California desert's siren call and wished to see into its mysterious past, or learn the fate of its many adventurers both historical and contemporary, read on!

In the pages ahead, author Choral Pepper writes in the narrative tradition of early twentieth century enthusiasts such as J. Smeaton Chase, the wide-ranging horseman who chronicled his adventures in *California Desert Trails*, novelist Harold Bell Wright and his *The Winning of Barbara Worth*, and explorer-writer George Wharton James, best known for *The Wonders of the Colorado Desert*. In this book, Choral spins the tales of many familiar and lesser-known individuals, sites, and events throughout the region, moving freely through the veil separating historical facts and their interwoven legends.

Her vignettes and stories are grouped geographically into eight travel corridors in a clockwise arc from Imperial Valley, northerly through Anza-Borrego and the Salton Sea area to Palm Springs, and then easterly through the Joshua Tree area to the Colorado River, and south again to the Mexican border. The characters in these stories roam the desert freely, ignoring contemporary boundaries on maps in a demonstration of their own unbounded spirit. Please see the reading list for the major guidebooks to Colorado Desert areas. These books contain practical travel information for your own wide-ranging explorations.

Welcome to the Lore of the Southern California desert!

PREFACE

The major portion of this book is devoted to southern California's low desert, properly called the Colorado Desert, but we also have included portions of the Mojave, or high desert, that touch upon it.

The Colorado Desert consists of a rough nugget-shaped area which drains either into the Colorado River or the Salton Sea. It reaches westward from the Colorado River, which gave it its name, to Anza-Borrego Desert State Park and southward below Twenty-nine Palms to the Mexican border.

In the thirties, a black man named George Bright, newly retired from the Los Angeles fire department, bought some acreage with a natural well in a particularly bleak section of the California desert and proceeded to build his house of dreams. Constructed of white painted cement blocks, it was visible from miles around; the sort of place that would electrify the hair of an architect of the let-the-building-blend-with-the-site school of thought. Actually, it was quite elaborate for the time and place, with three bathrooms each tiled in a different color, a penthouse on top of its second story and a red tile roof. But the piece de resistance was the proud home-owner's idea of installing a different colored window in each room.

Now as he lay in his various bedrooms, George Bright could look from his varicolored windows and hue the desert according to mood. The room with window glass of bright blue produced a permanently cool desert dawn. From another room bright red glass cast a rosy sunset glow over cacti, sky, and distant mountains. In yet another room with windows of chartreuse green, the desert grew lush and tropical, even miasmic.

This distinctive feature George Bright considered his greatest of decorative coups. He had no need to travel. He could produce the feel of any climate or geography right there within his own walls. And that is pretty much the way most desert-savvy individuals view the entire span of southern California's desert, but we find variety through awareness of what lies beyond the highway, rather than through tinted glass.

No one alive can boast of having explored the whole of the southern California desert. It is a region in which paradoxes of nature and enigmatic topography have compounded over a period of some fifteen million years to compose a soliloquy of enchantment unmatched by any other kind of land. This book focuses upon the wealth of legends and mysteries born within its boundaries.

Elevations vary from 4,505 feet high at the crest of Chuckwalla Mountain to 235 feet below sea level at the Salton Sea. At any elevation it is almost impossible during summer months for the average person to walk more than five miles in hot desert sun without water, and survive. Off-highway trails are infrequently patrolled. Car tracks do not always mean the ground is safe. An experienced explorer in this surprising desert never travels without two things: a shovel for getting his automobile out of sand and water.

Readers will find numerous references to Desert Magazine, a publication that covered every aspect of the desert — history, legend, lore, archaeology, culture, geology, flora and fauna. I purchased it in 1963 and edited it until I sold it in 1970. Working on the magazine proved to be a unique experience in my life. Most of the material and desert awareness that prompted this book was garnered from personal experience stimulated by reader's letters and contributing writers.

Retracing favorite desert trails for this book has given me enormous pleasure.

Choral Pepper
Coronado,California

ACKNOWLEDGMENTS

I wish that I could individually thank the scores of former *Desert Magazine* readers and contributing writers whose letters and articles I have drawn from freely in assimilating material for this book. I am also grateful for the support of the late Jack Pepper and my son Trent Lowe who organized so many desert explorations during the years we published the magazine.

I also am beholden to the scientists, botanists, story-tellers, archaeologists, anthropologists and park rangers—past and present—who contributed so much to my understanding and ability to relate to this most intriguing of all lands, the desert. I hope that in some small way this book will give back a worthy part of all that I have taken in.

I am grateful that Sunbelt's president and publisher, Diana and Lowell Lindsay, perceived a need for a book to perpetuate the mystique of the desert and chose me to write it. I also appreciate Publication Manager Nancy Smith's enthusiastic help with the book's first edition and now Sunbelt's Fred Noce's cooperation and friendship with this revised edition.

Imperial Valley Area

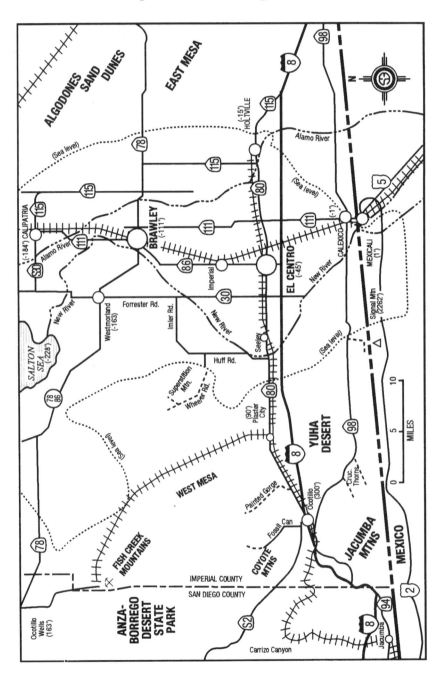

CHAPTER 1
IMPERIAL VALLEY AREA

IN THE GEOLOGIC BEGINNING

In earlier times, a shallow arm of the Gulf of California penetrated the Salton Trough as far north as Indio, possibly even reaching up to San Gorgonio Pass above Palm Springs. Near the shore of this vast, warm sea, oyster beds and shellfish flourished. Then, during post-glacial times, a raging silt-laden river from the northeast carved the Grand Canyon and funneled its load along the present boundary separating Alta and Baja California. As it emptied into the shallow waters of the Gulf of California, its accumulated silt became a delta-dike which separated the waters of the gulf from those imprisoned in the Salton Trough.

Slowly, through evaporation and dilution with fresh water, this captive inland sea disappeared, but later, further sediments from mountains framing the valley and on-again, off-again floods from the rampant Colorado River caused new fresh water lakes to form. These flourished and disappeared in turn over a period of about five million years, at times overlaying the trough with fresh water lakes.

The weight from these over burdens caused the earth's crust below to dimple and fold. Molten magmas pushed upward through weak spots and pressured lavas oozed along conduits of basement granites. As layered sediments writhed and buckled, further weakenings in the foundation occurred. Because of these movements, earthquakes resulted, causing cracks, or faults, up to many miles deep through the earth's crust to the hot, squishy mantle below. One of these, the San Andreas fault line, is clearly discernable in a number of areas between Desert Hot Springs and the mud hills that rise above the ancient beachline on the eastern shore of Salton Sea.

THE SEA RETURNS IN OUR TIME

The whole of inhabited Imperial Valley owes its existence to an outfit called The California Development Company. In 1900, promoters of the project enticed some twelve thousand persons to invest in this below-sea level desert with the promise that Colorado River water diverted by gravity through an old river channel would "make the desert bloom like a rose." They were right. It cost a bundle of

Imperial Valley.   The flood of 1905, with railroad tracks in right foreground. Courtesy of of San Diego Historical Society.

dollars, a number of reputations, engineering failures due to poor judgment and scores of flooded victims when the Colorado went on a rampage, but it turned out all right.

The father of this creative project was Dr. Oliver Meredith Wozencraft, a medical man from San Francisco who became infatuated with the mysterious Salton Sink and developed an obsession that it could be put to productive use. The idea was not entirely new, however. Dr. William Blake, geologist with a U.S. Government expedition, stood on the then dry shores of an ancient Lake Cahuilla in 1853 and had a similar idea when he noted that Cahuilla Indians were raising abundant crops of corn, barley, and vegetables in areas fed by springs. He wrote in his report, "if a supply of water could be obtained for irrigation, the greater part of the desert could yield crops of any kind... by deepening the channel of the New River or cutting a canal so low that the water of the Colorado would enter at all seasons." Sadly, neither Wozencraft nor Blake lived to see it happen.

It took Charles R. Rockwood, an engineer, who came along in 1892 to succeed in raising the necessary amount of capital. In 1902, the project finally got underway. Then, in 1905, all hell broke loose. Owing to careless construction of its head-gate, the old Alamo River channel, employed to carry the irrigation water, silted up and the Colorado forced another entry into Imperial Valley from below the Mexico line. The whole of waters, gathered from Utah, Wyoming, Colorado, New Mexico, Arizona and California, that fed into the Colorado erupted into a mile-wide breach remaking two almost forgotten rivers, the New and the Alamo.

Mexicali and Calexico were washed away. The town of Salton and its salt works in the Salton Sink were inundated on the floor of a rising in land sea and nearly fifty miles of Southern Pacific Railroad track were carried away, not to mention the acres of farmland destroyed. Because of the enormous revenue-producing freight traffic of Imperial Valley produce, the Southern Pacific Railroad came into the act. E. H. Harriman, president of the railroad, poured over four million dollars into various attempts to control the flood. His sixth attempt appeared to succeed. But not for long.

A year later an even more devastating breach occurred. Again the entire output of the Colorado came roaring into Salton Sea. This new catastrophe happened so suddenly that levee crews working below the break were marooned and had to be rescued by the *Searchlight,* a river steamer that served Colorado River mines between Yuma and Nevada. Before the craft could return to its base, however, the water had turned entirely toward the Salton Sea, leaving the steamer grounded in the dry stream bed.

This last devastation was followed by the San Francisco earthquake, an equally financially ruinous calamity faced by the Southern Pacific. Harriman had no more money to devote to saving Imperial Valley.

The farmers then took up the responsibility. They held mass meetings and obtained pledges for $950,000 from local water and power companies and the California-Mexico Land and Cattle Company, but the money was never collected.

Imperial Valley. *Dynamiting New River to divert direction of rapid headward erosion to save Mexicali and Calexico, 6/29/1906. Photo by Estella Falla, courtesy of Imperial County Historical Society.*

Desperate telegrams poured into the White House upon President Theodore Roosevelt. Congress had that very day adjourned. Unable to command financial aid from the Reclamation Service without congressional authority, Roosevelt responded with characteristic promptness. Taking decisive action upon his own responsibility, he personally contacted Harriman and assured him that the government would reimburse the railroad if Harriman would put men to work repairing the damage at once. Harriman ordered his chief engineer to "close that break at all costs." Work begun that same day was completed successfully a year later.

Harriman assumed this financial burden only upon the assurance of the President that the railroad would be reimbursed by the government, but this was never done. The railroad submitted a bill for $1,663,130, a mere fraction of the funds it had expended on other attempts to control the waters. It was introduced in Congress and referred to the Committee on Claims. Hearings were held and special commissions were appointed. At last the commission concluded that the Southern Pacific might legally be reimbursed, but only for twenty percent of the money spent.

Still no action was taken by Congress. Two years later, a bill was introduced reducing further the amount outstanding. The House

Imperial Valley.   *Views of Hind Dam, just south of the California border in Mexico at the site of the main break. The steamer Searchlight is seen in the river channel behind the tracks across the newly filled dike. Photo by Estella Falla, courtesy of Imperial County Historical Society.*

committee made a favorable report, but the opposition party in the House refused to pass the bill.

In the minds of people of Imperial Valley, the unpaid bill still remains a moral obligation unsatisfied by the U.S. Government.

In 1969 the sea faced a serious problem. Salt from Colorado River water combined with that used for agriculture in surrounding lands and funneled back into the riverbed to flow into Salton Sea posed a threat to recreation and fishing. Working together, the Salton Sea Recreation Department and Imperial Valley Irrigation District increased the amounts of fairly clean water now being used in the valley to stabilize the salt content. That danger appeared to be over when another arose. Although there is no exit to carry Salton Sea water to the ocean, it was expected that evaporation at the rate of six feet per year with the same amount of water entering the sea from farm lands would maintain sea water at a safe level. However, the amount of agricultural runoff depends upon weather and the kind of crops planted. In 1952, with the sea rising about one foot a year, floods all but annihilated some of the beach resorts. Since then the level has remained fairly level although a continuous battle is waged between ranchers and the Imperial Irrigation District over its control.

EL CENTRO

Founded in 1905 by W. F. Holt, an early developer, this largest of Imperial Valley towns first gained importance as a stop on the Southern Pacific rail line, but in recent years has grown because of

El Centro. *Mr. W.F. Holt, seated in the first passenger car of the Holton Interurban Railway. Photo courtesy of Imperial County Historical Society.*

Imperial Valley.
Looking down the
deep channel of
New River, washed
out through the
town site of
Calexico during
the great break
in the Colorado
in 1905. Photo
courtesy of
Imperial County
Historical Society.

its location on Interstate 8. Green fields surround it and a pungent earthy smell testifies to its ranking as one of the richest farming areas in the world. Tomatoes, sugar beets, cotton, melons and lettuce are among its crops.

EL CENTRO'S LOST SHIP LEGEND

It wouldn't be fair to El Centro to depart without recounting its contribution to lost ship treasures. An interview with the old-timer who found it, as told by the late desert historian Harold Weight, may bear more credence than others recounted later in this book.

It was in 1907 that young Elmer Carver, then seventeen, had been hired by a farmer named Nels Jacobson to keep an eye on the ranch and guard his wife while Jacobson made a business trip to Los Angeles. In making a tour of the ranch, some unusually heavy planks used for a hog pen aroused the boy's curiosity. Hefty wood like that was precious in desert land, especially for such a menial use. Two to three inches thick, eighteen inches wide and up to thirty feet long, the planks were fastened by iron bolts through bored holes, rather than nailed together as was customary.

That night at dinner with Mrs. Jacobson, he brought up the subject. The planks had come from an old boat once partially buried in a hill behind the house, she explained. The following morning Carver investigated further. What he found were additional immense timbers with the ribs of a boat still intact; so aged the wood appeared petrified. So far as he could tell, no iron had been used in its construction.

In time he had gained Mrs. Jacobson's total confidence. From within the mysterious boat, she later confided, Mr. Jacobson had recovered an iron chest filled with jewels. She estimated that a red ruby she showed to Carver was worth all the other jewels together. Among the others, which her husband was conspiring to sell to a pawnbroker in Los Angeles, were some emeralds and a golden crucifix set with sapphires.

After Jacobson's return there was no need to retain Carver, so the young man left the area to find steady work.

In trying to track the tale's veracity, Weight discovered an historical account of early settlers which referred to one Nels Jacobson as "a well-known rancher who came to Imperial with $4000 and left seven years later with $137,350."

BRAWLEY ORIGINS AND OSTRICHES

Much has happened to Brawley, north of El Centro, since its inception in 1902. At that time a Mr. Braley from Los Angeles, for whom the purchasers of his land had hoped to name their new town, declined the honor, declaring that he would not have his name associated with a project doomed to failure. Like a jilted bride whose linen had already been monogrammed, the township had grown accustomed to the name. To solve its dilemma, a member of the township committee remembered a friend in Chicago with the similar name of Brawley. He suggested that they name the town after him.

Strangely enough, the real Mr. Brawley never set foot in his town. The community itself, though, is very definitely there. A commercial center for stockgrowers, farmers and cross-country motorists, it and its close neighbor El Centro are Imperial County's biggest cities. Brawley's Cattle Call Rodeo celebrated annually is a popular two-day attraction each November.

There was a time here when herds of ostriches vied with those of cattle. That was in 1915 when one Lord Mosley stocked a farm with twenty-two-hundred of the long-legged, feisty birds. Plumes at $350 per pound were in great demand for fashionable hats and fans. Thus the British nobleman decided to give dealers in South Africa and Australia some competition. All went well so long as zoological gardens and glamorous ladies clamored for the dramatic vertebrate, but that suddenly ended with World War I. Ostrich feathers were "out;" art nouveau, flapper headbands and skinny short skirts were "in." The price of plumes dropped to $3.30 per pound. Lord Mosley dropped dead and the thousands of elegant birds he had kept on his Brawley farm were slaughtered.

Brawley. *Lord Mosley's ostriches being unloaded from a freight car. Photo courtesy of Imperial County Historical Society.*

PIONEER MUSEUM

Located off Exit I-8 at Hwy 111, then north to Ira Aten Road, this unusual museum is dedicated to preserving the life histories of the region's early settlers. Its eclectic accumulation of artifacts reflects the broad ethnic population that induced this arid region to "bloom like a rose."

Among them were Koreans, Swiss, African Americans, Chinese, East Indians, Filipinos, French, Greeks, Mexicans, Italians, Japanese, Lebanese, and Portuguese—a remarkable demonstration of immigrants from around the world each making a unique contribution to the cultivation of this once harsh land. The museum houses galleries depicting the use of various implements employed by early settlers to make their new home habitable.

SUPERSTITION MOUNTAIN— AN AZTLAN CONTENDER

Off to the west of Brawley rises Superstition Mountain, looking like a frosted dune because of its sandy mantle. Much mystery surrounds the mountain. Indians shunned it because of weird noises that issued from its interior. Prison convicts once stationed at a rock-crushing mill adjacent to it also told strange stories of moans and rumblings at night. While the mountain appears to be composed of sand, it actually consists of a granitic rock mass, filled with caves, joints and faults. Perhaps these creak and groan when desert winds shift the weight of sand above.

In 1965 a California graduate geologist, who also was a member of the California Bar Association, introduced a provocative concept. After years of searching throughout Mexico and the Southwest for the mysterious Aztec homeland described in the pre-Columbian Codex Boturini, Ralph Caine concluded that this seemingly insignificant range called the Superstitions was in reality the fabled Aztlan from whence came the Aztec nation. Caine built a strong case. Some of his colleagues took it seriously; others praised his imagination.

According to the Aztec calendar, in the year one this highly civilized tribe, called the Crane People, began their wanderings from a homeland far to the north of Mexico. An ancient codex describes this place, the Vale of Aztlan (place of reeds and herons), as an island with seven caves amid a lake surrounded by mountains and much swampy land.

Since 1885 historians have variously located Aztlan from Texas to California and from the great Salt Lake in Utah to Panama. Until Caine arrived at his conclusion, it was generally conceded that Aztlan had never been found. Caine contends that the best possible clues are the Aztec's recorded description of the place itself and legends of creation which the Pueblo Indians of the Southwest had in common with the Aztecs.

According to those legends, mother earth gave birth to their early ancestors in a dark underground world (cave) surrounded by land-locked waters. The vast cavern was roofed by a tremendous stone; "solid and resting upon the earth like an inverted bowl." Mountains to the west were blue, those to the north red, ones to the south white, with yellow to the east. Desert naturalist Lowell Lindsay suggests a regional parallel: yellowish Algodones sand dunes to the east; reddish sandstones of Mecca Hills to the north (or perhaps Red Rock Canyon in the Fish Creek Mountains); bluish Laguna Mountains to the west, and snow-capped Sierra San Pedro Martir (Baja's highest mountains) to the south.

In his book *Aztlan*, Caine reveals further clues derived from Pueblo Indian legends. In the lower level of this cave lived a water serpent who caused the floods and earthquakes that ultimately drove the Indians from the cave world. A severe earth shock crumbled their walls and water in the lake began to disappear, leaving soft marshy ground around its perimeter which eventually hardened into rock. Due to this last catastrophe, they had to dig out of their cave world before the rock overhang fell. After this final emergence into the "upper world," the Indians migrated eastward "across a great river" (Colorado River). An almost identical passage appears in the retraced migration route for Aztec souls returning back to their cave heaven after death.

Moreover, both Aztec and Pueblo Indians share a legend about one of their most important gods, Montezuma. These merge in an account of the Aztec emperor's priceless hoard of gold being dispatched to the ancient cave home far to the north to escape Cortez' plundering of Mexico City.

Solid evidence suggests that Superstition Mountain may very well be the real Aztlan. It once jutted into the great Lake Cahuilla, indicated by white calcium carbonate deposits marking a shoreline against surrounding mountain ranges. Protruding above the surface of those waters near the western shore would have been a peninsular mass consisting of Superstition Mountain and its associated hills. And most importantly, this relic island consists of a solid granitic "stone cover, like an inverted bowl" over fifty feet thick, resting upon lower sediments due to the fault rift character of the district. This is a very active seismic area as a result of its location in the San Jacinto Fault Zone, said to be historically the most active in California.

Some of this mysterious site that has mesmerized so many desert wanderers is closed to the public and is being used as an ordnance test range. Public access is from Wheeler Road, west from Huff Road, northwest of Seeley. See AAA map "Imperial County."

SEELEY AND THE NEW RIVER

The town of Seeley lies west of El Centro where S-80 crosses over New River. Little water is carried in the channel these days, but in the 1800s passing emigrants who happened to be camped there

Seeley. Looking South up New River from the new bridge of the San Diego and Arizona Railway, at Seeley. Signal Mountain in distant background. Photo courtesy of Imperial County Historical Society.

when the ravine suddenly filled with water hailed it as a miracle of Divine Providence. The phenomenon was, of course, a result of the Colorado River's periodic overflow that spun off into Volcano Lake in Baja California via the Rio Paredones, a tributary of the Colorado, and thence to New River

This on-again off-again schedule of New River changed with the subsequent controlling of the Colorado, but not before the disastrous flood season of 1906 had completely eliminated a town called Silsby and a group of adobes near a former stage stop known as Indian Wells (not to be confused with the present town of that name), located along its banks.

An amusing lost treasure legend grew up around the old stage stop. In 1906 a band of five men held up a detachment of cavalry guarding a payroll of $9,000 in gold destined for Fort Yuma. Four of the five men were apprehended and shot, but the fifth, a sharp-shooting gambler who affected a monocle and was known as "Endless Ed," escaped and was never seen again in the desert. At the time, there was speculation that he cached the loot near Indian Wells, the old stage stop, intending to return for it at a safer time. If so, it is still where he left it and remains for divers in New River to find.

SIGNAL MOUNTAIN AND THE ROBBERS' TREASURE CACHE

Looking to the south, conical Signal Mountain looms up against the horizon. Dirt roads through washes frequently are impassable following storms and deep sand at other times is a hazard. But, if the time is right, there are several off-highway sites en route to it that are of historical and geological significance.

As for the steep-sided mountain itself, it is obvious even today why Juan Bautista de Anza dubbed it *El Cero del Imposible*, the impossible mountain. When approaching it on his 1774 trek, he was forced to turn back and choose a different route. Months later, by skirting the dunes to the south, he advanced again toward this landmark and made it. Since then Signal Mountain, sprawled across the Mexican-U.S. border, has served as a beacon to desert travelers.

Old mines pock its pyramidal sides and treasure seekers make frequent forays to look for Indian gold, but the legend that inspires them is probably of recent vintage. The Cocopahs and Yuman tribes were supposed to have met in a battle many moons ago which resulted in the Cocopahs escaping to Signal Mountain with their injured chief and a fortune of gold confiscated from the enemy, which they buried near the landmark mountain. However, early Indians were not all that interested in gold. It took the white man to introduce them to such glittery values.

A more probable Signal Mountain fable concerns a cave laden with stolen loot located more or less directly on the international boundary. Its approximate burial ground was revealed to Joe Long, a local farmer, by an old one-legged worker who confessed to having once been a member of a band of robbers.

After one of their thieving forays the gang was apprehended by the posse, but managed to escape to a hideaway cave—a cave so large that it accommodated two buckboards. One member of the gang had been shot during the ruckus so the robbers left his corpse among a stock of rifles on one wagon and loaded the other with jewelry, bullion, gold coins and various spoils of plunder. They then concealed the cave's entrance and blew up the surrounding area with dynamite, hoping to return later to collect the loot.

A member of the posse was a former Imperial County fire marshall named Rudy Medina. He later confirmed that one by one the robbers were caught and killed, except for the old duffer known to Joe Long. A wound that ultimately resulted in the amputation of the robber's leg had caused him to separate from the fleeing gang. By the time he was found, wrath over the incident had ebbed and his life was spared. Instead of dying with his boot on, he was sentenced to twenty years in jail.

It was after his release around 1920 that he gave Joe Long directions to the canyon that held the cave. Long and his friends searched for it, as have countless other lost treasure buffs including desert writer Peter Odens. Long himself found a wagon wheel and bones of a man. His son on a later search recovered a fuse and some black powder. Odens found a few pieces of timber and a piece of rubber from a drive belt. No one yet has found the stolen riches secreted in "The Robbers' Cache."

YUHA DESERT—AN ANCIENT SEA AND HISTORIC WELL

This writer's family cherishes great memories of the Yuha Desert. Not being part of a government park system, it is a place where you can hear coyotes sing in a campsite "far from the madding crowd." I like that.

Its badlands to the south of the basin harbor myriad fish and shellfish fossils, some unrecognized today, that were deposited when this region was part of the sea. There used to be petrified driftwood logs here, too, but they have been carried away by collectors and few, if any, remain. Sand concretions are still around, though, some resembling dinner plates, others drumsticks, dumb-bells, flowers, and fruit.

Later, overland stages sometimes followed this route, stopping at Yuha Well to water their teams. Traces of the old Butterfield trail continue on directly west to Coyote Wells that parallels this border route to the north.

Another marked road in the Yuha Desert runs south into the petrified oyster beds. One of the most unusual spectacles in the low desert, this vast oyster shell bed once lay at the bottom of an ancient sea. No midgets, the oysters average about six to eight inches across. Scientists say that they lived toward the end of the Miocene period, about five million years ago. As a result of their studies, we have a fairly accurate picture of this region at that time. In the midst of a relatively shallow sea, Coyote Mountain formed an island of granite and metamorphic rocks. Balmy breezes warmed the tropical air, evidenced by fossil reefs, while sharks swam in the sea and prehistoric forms of horse and camel roamed the shore.

Initially the oyster beds raised more questions than they answered with their age a major subject for debate. Some paleontologists dated them from Cretaceous times more than 70 million years ago; others to the early Pliocene period about 4 thousand years ago. To confound the mystery, geologists discovered that the fossil shells' closest living relatives were in the Atlantic Ocean rather than off the California coast!

An expedition of the California Academy of Science to the Gulf of California in 1921 cleared up that mystery by establishing that the ancient shells were related to Gulf species which in many ways resemble marine life in the Atlantic more closely than that in the Pacific. Descendents of the fossil forms live today in warm Gulf waters almost unchanged from their ancestors.

A short distance west of the oyster beds is Yuha Well. When this bleak, desolate basin of modified sand hills greeted Anza on his second cross-country attempt, he despaired of carrying on further until signs of the spring appeared. He called it Pozo de Santa *Rosa de las Lajas*, "Well of St. Rose of the Flat Stones," in reference to the platter-like concretions distinctive to the area.

CRUCIFIXION THORN

A sign on Highway 98 near the Vista De Anza Monument indicates an area in which Crucifixion Thorn grows, a rare desert species reputed to be the one used to crown the head of Christ at the time of his crucifixion. Actually, it is not the same. A near-relative to the Chinese Tree of Heaven, this one is known to botanists as *Castela emoryi*. Its dense cluster of nutlike fruit made good donkey feed, but otherwise was useless to man.

PLASTER CITY AND PAINTED GORGE

When gypsum deposits were discovered in Fish Creek Mountains, some twenty-five miles away, an El Centro druggist saw the potential and organized a company to develop them. The company eventually sold out to U.S. Gypsum and today's modern plant arose. Roughly ten percent of the national output of gypsum is gleaned from Fish Creek mines each year. It is the largest such mine in the U.S.

West of Plaster City, start looking for a marked graded road leading north to a scenic geologic marvel popular with photographers and picnickers. Don't be deceived by the flat desert studded with ocotillo, desert-varnished rocks and occasional smoke trees leading into it. They are no indication of the vivid patchwork of color that lies seven miles along the trail. Some of the Painted

Painted Gorge.   Through the years this has been a fascinating area to explore.–CP.

Gorge is formed of coral reefs that contain oysters so well preserved you expect to find living mollusks dwelling inside of them. Look and enjoy but don't collect them.

Secluded camping coves break off from the graded road along the way. Passenger cars can make it well into the canyon, but even four-wheel-drivers will choose to hike over the last part to the canyon's colorful upper reaches. This is definitely a scenic spot worth a visit.

CARRIZO CANYON AND REEDY'S LOST GOLD

In 1967 I received a letter from Joe Reedy, a *Desert Magazine* reader, lamenting that old age had finally arrested his efforts to locate the source of a gold find near the old San Diego and Arizona Eastern Railroad tracks some eight miles west of Ocotillo. He knew the gold was there because he had seen it; not on the ground, but in the hands of an El Centro farmer who had been paid the gold by an old prospector in exchange for milk, eggs, and past kindnesses.

Following directions given by the farmer, Reedy made six trips over a period of as many years looking for the lone palm and cache of prospector's tools that would put him on the track of the lost mine. He had found the palm, but not the tools or the gold. During a final trek, he stopped at the old Dos Cabezas railway station to inquire if anyone had been prospecting in the area.

The answer he received was revealing. Some years earlier an Indian had lived in one of the cabins by the station. Each morning the Indian walked to Tunnel 21 and each evening returned, a total distance of fourteen miles. After about ten weeks of this, the Indian asked the railroad worker for a ride in his motor car to Coyote Wells where he could catch a bus for San Diego. After the railroad man agreed to that, the Indian requested another favor. He wanted help in carrying his "stuff" from the cabin. The "stuff" was packed in a buckskin bag with a stick tied into the top. It took the strength of both men to lift it.

About a week later, this same Indian showed up in Julian, spending nuggets over the bar for liquor. Both the railroad worker and the bartender tried to find out where he had obtained his gold, but all the Indian would say was, "Tunnel 21."

Reedy immediately made a beeline for Tunnel 21, which turned out to be about one-quarter mile down the canyon from the lone palm where the other prospector had worked, although by this time the palm had disappeared. Reedy couldn't figure out then—and still couldn't—why he failed to find anything where two others had found so much.

I couldn't either so, accompanied by the late Jack Pepper and my young son Trent Lowe, we set forth with a topographical map, headed for the abandoned Dos Cabezas Station. One of the assets to having a Boy Scout in the family was that when we reached an impasse we could send Trent ahead on his trail bike to make reconnaissance. At last, after some rough driving and hiking along a rocky footpath, we spied our long-sought railroad tunnel. At least, we thought it was until we climbed close enough to discover the sign at its entrance read Tunnel 20, the wrong one.

According to our topo map, Tunnel 21 lay beyond a deep canyon on the other side of the mountain through which this one was cut. In spite of the hour growing perilously late, we were too close to our goal to give up. We climbed to the top "just to take a look," but what we saw demanded closer examination.

Descending on the other side from one sandstone ledge to another, we finally looked down into a boulder-strewn, sandy wash blocked by an immense wall of fill which had been built up to provide a bed for the tracks. Where the tracks disappeared into the mountain on the opposite side of the wash, gaped the black cavity of Tunnel 21.

Extending from the floor of the canyon and cut through the rocky fill of the track bed, was a drainage tunnel designed as an outlet for water rushing down the canyon during flash floods. When we reached the floor of the canyon, we peered into the drainage tunnel. Square cut and about fifty-feet long, its top and sides were timbered and along its sandy floor were thick railroad ties placed at regular intervals.

Up the wash into which we had descended to locate the tunnel is where the old prospector's lone palm had once stood. We had left our metal detectors in the car and it was too late then to pursue the matter further. Still, there were no signs of mining in the area. I began to wonder if the nuggets the Indian displayed in Julian had been black-coated like the legendary Pegleg's, by any chance.

The more I thought about it as we drove home in the dark, the more perplexed I became. In the office the next morning, I called Joe Reedy.

As if I were some kind of idiot for asking, he answered, "Of course the nuggets were gold colored, as gold nuggets always are!"

"Those boulders around Tunnel 21 didn't look very gold-bearing to me," I persisted. "How far from the tunnel do you think the mine was located?"

"The gold didn't come from a mine. It was placer gold, washed down that canyon from somewhere above."

"Why, then, didn't it wash right on through the drainage tunnel and down the deep canyon on the other side?" I asked.

"Because gold is heavier than sand," he patiently explained. This fact opened up a whole new premise in my mind. Gold would have dropped to the bottom and been trapped between those ties that lay in the bottom of the drainage tunnel!

Perhaps it is just as well that we didn't think of that while we were there. Although Joe Reedy's lost gold lies close to the park boundary, which was not a protected area when he searched, it lay within the confines of Anza-Borrego Desert State Park by the time we looked. What is found in the park, must remain in the park.

The tropical Storm Kathleen devastated the old San Diego and Arizona Railroad in January of 1976 and no doubt swept away or buried any remains of Reedy's unclaimed gold. The railroad reopened briefly in 1981, but recurring storms soon forced a permanent closure—and closed the door on a lost gold legend.

CALEXICO—A FUTURE SEAPORT?

Lying south of El Centro, Calexico's name is a combination of California and Mexico, responded to in kind by the Mexicans who named its sister city on their side of the border "Mexicali."

Originally a tent city erected in the 1900s to serve builders of the first canal built from the Colorado River in Mexico to Imperial Valley, Calexico was situated upon a 150-acre tract owned by George Chaffrey, one of the promoters of the valley irrigation project. The first adobe to replace tents, now the post office, arose in 1901.

In its early days, Calexico was chiefly a weekend town filled with saloons and bawdy houses frequented by Imperial Valley workers. Today, however, it has thrown off the tawdry mantle and is now an attractive community with a strong Mexican accent. Overhangs cover streets in the old part of town, run-down, but more picturesque than the neon-lighted modern buildings that now house a plethora of Mexican car insurance salesrooms and eating places.

The old De Anza Hotel on 4th Street was a center for Hollywood galas during the Prohibition era when film stars stayed there to gambol and gamble in Mexicali directly across the border. With the repeal of Prohibition in 1931 and subsequent banning of gambling in Mexico, the hotel was more or less abandoned. It was restored in 1966 by Harold H. Johnson, a local rancher, who recovered many of the original custom-made furnishings. Murals were restored and once again gaslight chandeliers brought charm to the old hotel. Today, however, it must compete with modern, attractive motor lodges in the area.

Grandiose dreamers are legion on the desert. Without them the All American Canal would not have made Imperial Valley "bloom like a rose" nor would Palm Springs have developed into the most famous health spa in the world. There is still another dream, yet to be realized, that could bring about enormous change to the face of the desert. The plan for a saltwater seaport was born in 1932 when Henry J. Kaiser, the steel magnate, joined up with the U.S. State Department to conceive a canal from the Gulf of California to the Mexicali/Calexico area. Kaiser, who was in the process of building his steel mill at Fontana, was interested in a port that would accommodate large ships to facilitate shipping his goods to Japan. The State Department's incentive was a plan, later abandoned, to build a railroad line from Spokane, Washington south for defense purposes.

There are locals who still consider the port a viable idea. A canal could convey water from the gulf for twenty-five miles to a point west of Mt. Signal, which rises above the border of the U.S. and Mexico. The project would have to be a joint enterprise with Mexico, of course, but in view of other recent joint projects, both countries would benefit. Costs could be amortized by extensive use of the canal for fishing and boating concessions as well as by industry attracted to both sides of the border. In addition, low cost power could be produced similar to the hydroelectric drops in the All-American Canal.

The initial plan projected that devastating gulf tides could be controlled with four locks, but a more advanced plan required only one lock at the entrance to the canal where it met Laguna Salada. Although Kaiser's enthusiasm waned when he became involved in World War II efforts, there was a brief revival of interest in 1968 when a commission composed of seven Mexicans and four U.S. members gave it further consideration. At that time James T. Ramey, commissioner of the Atomic Energy commission that would be called upon to dig the canal, declared that the new waterway should be some three hundred feet wide and seventy-five feet deep. Waters from the gulf would then form an inland sea some thirty-five miles long and fifteen miles wide within Laguna Salada. It was also suggested that when the salinity of Salton Sea became a problem, canal water could be utilized to augment the sea. At that time the Mexican Government agreed to make it a free port, despite objections from the Mexican Navy fearing the port might lay Mexico open to attacks.

Then, as with most dreams conceived ahead of their time, nothing happened. With the quickening pace of cooperation evident between our border countries today, however, cruise passengers bound for the south might someday be boarding in Calexico!

Salton Sea and Environs

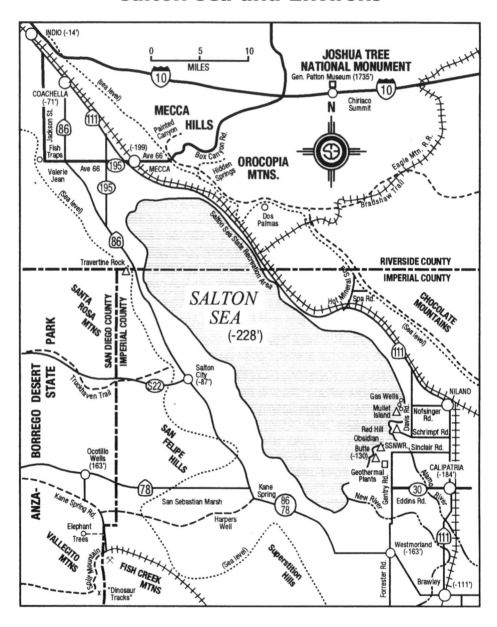

CHAPTER 2
SALTON SEA AND ENVIRONS

NEW SEA IN AN OLD LAND

Salton Sea has come a long way in a short time. Less than a century ago, it was not even there. Today, its waters support boat regattas, fish derbies, water skiers, and swimmers. Its shores are dotted with marinas, vacation houses, and resorts. Its history includes Pegleg's back gold, Indian legends, lost mines, an enigmatic murder mystery still debated and ancient trails, as well as incredible geological and botanical mysteries.

The comparatively recent creation of Salton Sea by the runaway Colorado River was far from the first time an inland sea had filled the basin. When Dr. William Blake, a geologist with an early exploring party, noted deposits of travertine marking the height of beachlines along the side of the Santa Rosas framing the west side of the Salton Sink, he determined that an ancient sea called Lake Cahuilla had more than once filled the basin. Then gradually, through evaporation, the land-locked lakes had disappeared, only to be refilled again whenever the fickle Colorado jumped her banks. Fossil deposits have been found as high as a thousand feet above the floor of the desert and conch shells were so numerous that the valley was originally called Conchilla Valley (Due to an error in spelling, it is now called Coachella Valley).

What might have been inundated or swept away by earlier floods will never be known. We do know that a town called Salton disappeared in the flood of 1905-6 and with it the New Liverpool Salt Works with railroad tracks, freight cars, and residences that housed workers. On certain days, boaters report seeing relics of this industry underwater.

Secondary only to the flood itself was the chagrin of old-timers when they found their favorite hunting ground for the fabled Pegleg Smith's lost gold inundated. Near the south shore of Salton Sea were three volcanic buttes covered with pumice stone. One of these was believed to be the eminence upon which old Pegleg found his gold, according to George Wharton James, the indefatigable desert chronicler who lamented the loss in 1906. Recent evidence, however, suggests that James lamented in vain. Wherever it was that Pegleg found his gold, this writer has proof that it is not now under the Salton Sea.

The long, flat expanse of desert floor to the west of Salton Sea is deceptive. When you try to cross it in a four-wheel-drive vehicle or afoot, you learn that it is not flat at all. It is a maze of barrancas, arroyos, ravines and washes. And where it looks bleak and lifeless from the surface, down in those washes may be clouds of smoke trees filled with purple blooms in June, or bursts of yellow palo verde blossoms in Spring.

Wonderful legends tell of Spanish galleons and Viking ships that still may be found under desert sands, one of which gave birth to an old Indian legend.

COLLECTION OF PARADOXES

A collection of paradoxes, Salton Sea is a lake in which wood sinks, fish have gizzards like birds, rocks float, and vapors of dry ice at a minus-temperature bubble up through warm water.

The sinking wood is from ironwood trees that grew in the Salton Sink before it filled with water. The rock is volcanic pumice,

Salton Sea. *The plaque (now gone) on the monument, south side of Travertine Rock. August 1977.– LEL.*

found along its southeastern shore. The fish are mullets, a saltwater species that migrated from the Gulf of California into Salton Sea via the Colorado River. The dry ice is CO_2 rising from a natural spring under the sea near Niland.

An extinct Salton Sink oddity is a field of mud volcanoes, first noted in 1852 by Major Heintzelman. Surprised to see clouds of steam rising into the air, he investigated and discovered twenty-eight acres of eruptions shooting mud as high as forty feet. Caused by infiltration of water down to heated bedrock where it converted into steam and pressured up again, the mud volcanoes are only bubbles on the surface of the sea today.

Perhaps the greatest paradox of all, though, is that this is a sea below a sea. Its minus altitude is 227 feet below sea level. For that reason it exists as a sea today. During the heavy run-off in 1905, when the undammed channel of the Colorado River could no longer contain the torrential volume of water rushing through it, the surplus sought any cavity it could find. Thus gravity pulled it along ravines cut by former floods into the below-sea-level depression of the Salton Sink.

The deep crust of salt that forms the basin of the sink changed the chemistry of the fresh Colorado River water that created Salton Sea. Since then the sea has grown even more salty due to the leaching out of minerals from irrigation water dumped into it, maintaining a constant level. Boating enthusiasts are pleased with the high density because it makes boats move faster, but the game fish, corvina and sargo, and the small fish that feed them are putting up a battle to survive in salinity that exceeds that of the ocean. A related problem is the decaying of organic matter at the bottom of the sea during late summer months. This robs the water of oxygen and results in dead fish and algae which produce an unpleasant odor that interferes with recreation at that time.

LEGEND OF THE GREAT WHITE BIRD

Long ago a great flood came to the desert and everyone was forced to move up into the hills to await the leaving of the water. Almost every year in the time of the spring there was a flood, but this was the greatest flood of all and it lasted the longest time. One day, after the third dance had been held, there appeared a great bird with white wings that moved slowly across the top of the water, as if seeking a place to go ashore. When it lowered its great white wings, the Indians noticed what appeared to be ants on the back of the bird.

Salton Sea. *Photo by Walt Schmidtke, October, 1993.*

The tribe's medicine man made quick medicine to ward off evil spirits while curious Indians, hiding in rocky caves, watched the ants lower themselves into dark objects on the water and make their way to the shore. As they drew close, the Indians observed that the "ants" were men much as themselves, but with strangely white skin and hair bleached the color of corn tassels.

The strange men invaded canyons to cut down trees and carry them to the "birds" on the placid waters, but it was never able to free itself. Soon the waters went away and the great bird fell over on its side and died. The wind blew away its white wings and the body of the great bird slowly slid down the hill where wind buried it in the sand. Sometimes, though, the wind blew away sand to reveal the body of the great bird, but that was an omen of evil and no one dared draw near.

WEST SHORE AND MOUNTAINS

PEGLEG SMITH'S BLACK GOLD AND THE MAN WHO FOUND IT

No other lost gold legend has created the excitement of Pegleg Smith's black gold. So renowned was it, in fact, that after the Civil War, Peglegs must have been as prevalent as Smiths. Three of them turned up in different cities, all claiming to be the REAL Pegleg

Smith. One, however, boasted of a mine. Pegleg's find was not a mine; it was placer gold washed down from a lode. Of the other two, most Pegleg buffs have settled upon Thomas Long "Pegleg" Smith, a trapper, guide, Indian fighter and horse thief, with a wooden leg who discovered his black gold nuggets in 1829 while journeying from Yuma to Los Angeles via Warner's Ranch. Here, we shall deal with that one.

Striking out into unknown territory with one companion, their horses and a pack of skins to trade in Los Angeles, Pegleg was the first American to cross the Colorado Desert from Yuma to Warner Springs. Somewhere in the desolate region in which he found himself, he climbed one of three adjacent hills to take a sighting, on top of which lay a quantity of weighty black lumps which he assumed to be copper. He pocketed a few to show his companion waiting below, thinking that they might mold them into bullets if necessary. Upon finally arriving in Los Angeles, he displayed the "native copper" to a miner in a saloon and was astonished to learn that the rocks were covered with desert varnish, but underneath had a heart of gold. Through the years until he died in San Francisco, fortuneless at age sixty-five, Pegleg tramped the desert again and again in search of his black gold bonanza, always in vain.

More fortunate as both finder and keeper was a half-breed Indian who lived near Warner's Ranch on the northwestern fringe of the Anza-Borrego Desert in 1880. He used to go out in the desert and after four days return with enough gold to meet his immediate needs. Later, after he was knifed in a brawl, more than $4,000 worth of coarse black-coated gold was found in his bunk.

Then one day in 1965, while I was editor of *Desert Magazine*, I picked up a package at the post office addressed to me personally. In it were two cobbles of peculiar shape—one black as a chocolate-covered peanut cluster, the other shining gold—accompanied by a letter from the anonymous sender who signed himself "the man who found Pegleg's black gold."

The two stones which he had sent to establish his veracity were gold nuggets, one in the natural black state as found, the other polished. His letter began: "It is time once and for all to end the mystery, the speculation and the controversy. Almost ten years ago I found what has been known since 1852 as the 'burned black gold of the Pegleg.' Since the first discovery, I've brought out and sold a total of $313,650 black gold nuggets." (This, at a time when gold was worth $35 an ounce.)

As editor, I was obliged to suspect a hoax. The "mystery, speculation and controversy" had raged for 135 years. Lives and fortunes had been lost in fruitless efforts to find this bonanza. We were on the gold standard then with gold valued at only $35 an ounce, but his find still represented a mighty fortune.

The anonymous writer went on to explain how he had sold the nuggets to Canadian and Alaskan gold merchants after removing the black coating with acid. So I had them assayed and found the writer's appraisal true—seventy percent gold, twenty percent silver and ten percent copper. It was the copper molecules that oxidized to give the nuggets their black color.

"Mr. Pegleg," as we began to refer to the anonymous writer, offered to answer questions from readers and to include a nugget with each answer as authentication. His purpose was "to give hope to those hardy souls who have spent months and years of their lives searching for lost bonanzas."

Our Mr. Pegleg, however, was not a dedicated gold seeker. "I had driven into the low desert for a weekend of fresh air, good weather, some exercise, and a bit of rock hunting," he wrote, during which he had stopped to rest atop a small rise. Idly, he picked up a water-worn pebble from the black crust covering the rise and flipped it down the slope, like a marble. The third or fourth of these he picked up felt heavier than the others. After hefting it several

Hills Near Salton Sea. *Weekend prospectors search the southern California desert for a nugget of the famed Pegleg "black gold." Circa 1970.–CP*

times, he considered that its weight for its size indicated metal. With the blade of a pocket knife, he scraped the surface. Gold shown from underneath.

"I'll never know how long I sat there paralyzed with that first black gold nugget in my hand...," he wrote. He decided not to stake a claim, but kept returning to the spot over a ten year period with a metal detector until he had gathered all on the surface and within a few feet below.

This modern Pegleg's find set off a new wave of gold fever. I received phone calls and letters by the hundreds. Los Angeles television commentators came for interviews. Sun-baked prospectors in sand-scuffed shoes sidled into the office, certain we knew more than we were telling. Countless families from Los Angeles and San Diego stopped to examine the black gold nuggets on display in my office, hoping to match them on their own gold hunt. For Mr. Pegleg believed that still more would be uncovered by desert winds and storms.

A map from an early *Desert Magazine* outlining the area in which he found his gold accompanied his first letter. It lay within thirty miles of Salton Sea, but since Salton Sea is fifty miles long, that covers a lot of territory. Other clues included signs of volcanic activity, places seared by desert winds, and rocks gathered into a circle either by Indians or by nature. Many sought, but if anyone succeeded it was never confirmed. Black nuggets may rest there yet.

During the years I published *Desert Magazine*, the nuggets were displayed in our office for readers to see. When I sold the magazine, I felt that with one exception—a nugget addressed to me personally—they had been sent to our readers, so of course I left them. After that, they disappeared and I understand that no further nuggets were sent to the magazine.

Accounts of all the Peglophiles who have devoted years to a fruitless search for black gold, as well as some who inadvertently stumbled upon a few nuggets and then lost them, has filled countless books, many privately published. Here, and in later chapters, we will give credence to only a few of those observations or opinions that we consider relevant enough to share.

OLD SPANISH TRAIL AND BUCK'S BLACK GOLD THEORY

Before we leave "Pegleg" country in this area, the Marsh of San Sebastian, too, holds promise of treasure, but with a novel slant. The assay of our modern Mr. Pegleg's gold struck a familiar note in the memory of California historian Robert Buck, bolstered by the fact that this route had encompassed an old Spanish trail.

Buck was aware that almost all gold mined in Northern California's Mother Lode country contained ten to twenty percent silver alloy, but with one exception, none contained copper. That exception applied to a secret mining operation in Calaveras County which was carried on by the wealthy Peralta family of Sonora, Mexico, a few years prior to the discovery of gold at Sutter's Creek. It was black gold and the alloys were about twenty percent silver and ten percent copper.

The two Peralta sons who oversaw the operation made no attempt to process the nuggets in California. They preferred to send the gold in its natural black disguise by pack train over the long overland route to Sonora which passed through the central part of California, east of Los Angeles, then southward across the desert to what later became the boundary of Mexico and the United States.

A relevant incident recalled by Buck had appeared in an old Mexican California archive. In the early 1830s a large pack train carrying ore from the Peralta mine had set forth on its long journey to Sonora, accompanied by one of the Peralta sons. Succumbing to an urge for entertainment en route, the young man sent the slow-moving caravan ahead while he and a few companions detoured to San Francisco. After dallying there for three days, Peralta and his party hurried to catch up with the pack train, but when they finally arrived in Sonora, the caravan of ore-laden horses was not there. At first Peralta thought he had somehow overtaken them, but as time passed any hope of the pack trains safe arrival died.

Buck's theory, and one which the mysterious modern Pegleg considered plausible, was that the pack train was ambushed by Indians, who sought only the horses. After slaying the pack train attendants, the Indians cut loose the senseless load of black rocks and disappeared with the horses. Thus, the payload our Mr. Pegleg recovered so easily from the ground was that deposited by the lost Peralta caravan. This theory was further enhanced when our Mr. Pegleg mentioned in one of his letters that he had found an old Spanish silver belt buckle at the site of the black gold.

KANE SPRING AND THE
MARSH OF SAN SEBASTIAN

A dirt road west from Westmoreland leads to Harper's Well, which was the first water stop for early travelers on the Old County Road, now approximating Hwy 78. Anza named this area the "Marsh of San Sebastian" to honor his Indian guide, Sebastian Tarabal. When Fages

Old Kane Spring Road.–CP

was there two years earlier, in 1772, he had called it *Cineguita del Tular* or "little marsh of the tules." In 1853, this marsh where Carrizo and San Felipe creeks come together saved the lives of Blake's survey party. Then, about 1920, a flurry of water-well digging and oil well wildcatting took place and a boomtown named San Felipe City was lauded with much fanfare. Judging from the debris of broken pottery, charcoal from long-ago fires and chipped arrowheads, however, it would appear that the Marsh of San Sebastian was more successful at supporting ancient Indian villages than it was twentieth century ones. There are not even ruins to look at now.

Kane Spring, opposite the turnoff to Harper's Well, was another water hole used by early explorers and Indians. One of the local myths about Spanish galleons caught in the Salton Basin was launched here in 1890 when a prospector at Kane Spring asserted that he had seen one embedded in a nearby hill. Searches, however, failed to reveal it—and no wonder. Although controversial, it is commonly believed that lakes filling the basin during years of the Spanish exploration were fresh water from the runaway Colorado River and did not give entry to the Gulf of California. Fossilized ocean shells that appear here were deposited during an earlier age.

OCOTILLO WELLS AND ELEPHANT TREES

This community serves as the eastern gate to Anza-Borrego Desert State Park. Paved Split Mountain Road running south from the center of town leads to a number of interesting areas, among them one of the traditional choices for the most likely location for finding Pegleg's black gold.

As you travel along Split Mountain Road, take note of the variety of desert plants. Creosote is the most common, its dark green leaves and blackish stems easily distinguished against the light desert floor. The waxy coating on its small leaves slows water loss and helps to reflect heat. Unlike the ashy white burroweed, its common neighbor that drops its leaves to conserve water during dry periods, the creosote is an evergreen that can withstand up to a 70% water loss, greater than any other xerophyte of dry climate.

Although the prevalent ocotillo are armed with vicious spines, they do not belong to the cactus family. Encouraged by a good rain, blossoms unfurl at their tips like little red flags. Early settlers, who laced the canes together to make fences, were cheered when their fences took root and suddenly became decorative.

Most low desert washes are graced by the lovely smoke tree and its smaller cousin, the indigo bush, both names inspired by deep blue blossoms that appear in June. The smoke tree is a favored subject for desert artists. It really should be seen by moonlight to appreciate the full effect of feathery gray leaves that then appear more than ever like smoke. The ultimate in ethereal beauty, these members of the pea family grow only in areas periodically watered by flash floods. The hard outer coatings of their

Elephant Trees near Split Mountain and south of Ocotillo Wells.
Photo courtesy of Copley Books.

seeds must be abraded by water and sand action in order to germinate. They do not transplant, but have been grown successfully from seed.

Some six miles south of Ocotillo Wells on Split Mountain Road a marked turnoff leads to the Elephant Tree Discovery Trail. This rare, squatty ecological oddity, with malformed twiggy branches, flourishes along a mile-and-a-half trail amid barrel cactus, cholla, ocotillo, and smoke trees.

Botanists refused to believe that it existed until an expedition set forth to prove it in 1937. Early Indians, believing that the native American tree had medicinal properties, kept it hidden. The tree is more commonplace in Baja California.

OLD KANE SPRING ROAD—SLEEPING CIRCLES AND PEGLEG PLACERS

About two-and-a-half miles south of S-78 on Split Mountain Road, Old Kane Spring Road takes off to the west. This dirt road is also known as Pole Line Road. Eventually it joins S-78 inside Anza-Borrego Desert State Park. On low hills south of this road, scores of old-timers expected to find Mr. Pegleg's gold. All of the clues presented by the modern Pegleg gold finder are here—Indian rock circles, low hills, wind blown sand, low desert. Further, the original Pegleg got lost while trying to find a shortcut to Warner's Ranch from Yuma. Such a short cut along an old Indian trail was known to exist through Split Mountain close to the south.

Mysterious rock circles, noted by the modern Mr. Pegleg, lie atop many of the hills along the route of the Pole Line Road. The significance of the circles is unknown. In northern Indian areas similar circles have been called tepee circles, but desert Indians lived in temporary brush shelters or caves, not tepees. It is possible that the rings performed the function of a bank. We have noticed in undisturbed areas that often the rings contain little piles of quartz or other rocks that might have been worked into projectile points or used for tools. There may have been a superstition or Indian honor code that forbade poachers to remove anything contained within a rock circle. Along these foothills, bedrock mortars, caves, and an abundance of ironwood trees also recall a time when ancient Indian squaws winnowed black seeds from ironwood pods to grind into meal on their stone metates.

An oddball multiple barrel cactus may be seen in this area too. Normally barrel cacti, which expand and contract like an accordion during wet and dry periods, grow with a single stem, but here they are found in clusters. That their slimy, alkaline pulp is a source of drinking water is debatable, although thirsty jack-rabbits and bighorn sheep have been known to eat their flesh.

Those citing this region as a likely Pegleg gold area were encouraged by an article written for the *California Mining Journal* in 1954 by the late Harry Phillips, a mining engineer with lifetime experience in managing gold mines. I was so impressed by his knowledge of the desert that I contacted him to ask his opinion of the black gold find of our modern Pegleg.

"Black gold does exist in this district," he informed me, "in the same *salty phyllite schist* that exists in the California Mother Lode up north. During the Ice Age, when most of today's erosion features occurred, parts of this area were covered with forests and great rivers that provided milling and assorting action to produce gold placer deposits which washed down from higher elevations. It is possible that remnants of ancient old-channel placers exist, which may be detected by a marked red color due to heavy black iron associated with placer gold. All old channel gold is coated black. Much of the gold could be locked up in young conglomerate and caliche."

Harry Phillips had positive evidence of black gold here as well as in other locations in this approximate area. One incident he related concerned gold given to a doctor living at Warner Springs by an Indian whose life he had saved. When asked where the Indian had found his gold, the Indian took him to Pinyon Mountains, pointed easterly toward this area and said, "when wind blow, Indian pick up gold."

Hopefully the winds have uncovered new finds since Mr. Pegleg was there, but also hopefully, you will find your black gold outside of park borders, as it is illegal to remove anything natural from the park.

Phillips recalled yet another location just outside the park where placer gold had been found in quantity, namely south of Ocotillo in the vicinity of the old San Diego-Arizona-Eastern Railroad, as mentioned in the previous chapter. This area also eventually winds up within Anza-Borrego Desert State Park at Dos Cabezas, but when Mr. Pegleg found his black gold around 1954, the area was not yet included within confines of the park.

Both locations mentioned by Phillips had at one time or another been revealed as a source of black gold finds by Indians, although not in the quantity of the modern Mr. Pegleg's. One factor to consider in light of desert Indian reports of gold, is that their trails usually passed along the tops of ridges and mesas, only dipping into washes when necessary. So choose a nice day when wild-flowers are abloom in the spring and take your pick of the high roads. Except, of course, if you get lost. Then keep in mind that in nearly every instance if a wash is followed downward it eventually will lead to a route of travel, a road, habitation or water. A major exception to this down-wash rule would be Carrizo Creek in the Carrizo Badlands. There one would want to travel upwash, eventually to reach Hwy S-2.

SPLIT MOUNTAIN—DESERT VARNISH AND DINOSAUR TRACKS

Continuing south to the end of Split Mountain Road, you are in one of the most fascinating areas of the desert. The Fish Creek primitive camp lies within the fringe of park borders, but the gypsum mine at the end of the road does not. Many an early traveler lost his life in the maze of canyons and washes that wend westward along a four-wheel-drive road into Split Mountain. The trail once provided a shortcut between Carrizo Spring, Borrego Valley and San Felipe, all in Anza-Borrego Desert State Park. Pegleg gold prospectors like this area, too.

The black coating seen on rocks here, called desert varnish, occurs in desert regions all over the world, often on the faces of rocky cliffs as well as on rock covered ground. European scientists refer to it as *dunkel Riden* and believe it is caused when rain water soaks into the rock and is then brought back to the surface by capillary action of the sun. Here it evaporates, leaving a deposit of the

Wind Caves and "the phantom." Just south of Split Mountain, they are the site of fabled "dinosaur tracks" (actually erosional features).–LEL

chemicals with which it becomes charged according to the composition of the rock itself. If there is too much moisture, it departs the rock in liquid form and carries the salts with it. If there is too little moisture, salts are not dissolved to form the varnish. Consequently, in desert climates of little moisture, it can take many centuries to form. In areas where other evidence establishes a definite climatic pattern, it is possible to estimate the approximate ages of petroglyphs, prehistoric incised markings on rock surfaces.

A theory more popularly accepted by California scientists, however, was advanced by the late Jerry Laudermilk, a Pasadena scientist. He found that desert varnish is a lichen which attacks rocks containing iron and manganese. In rainy seasons, this decays and the iron and manganese pass into solution, re-precipitating on surrounding rocks of any kind. Continuing century after century and toasting under hot desert sun, it finally attains a rich *cafe au lait* color on its exposed side. The unexposed side remains natural. Actually, Laudermilk was able to create desert varnish under controlled conditions within a shorter period of time than previously thought possible.

Sometimes too much knowledge can be a killjoy, which proved true in the case of the dinosaur tracks. Old timers had a wonderful time tracking dinosaurs to their lairs up Split Mountain Gorge toward the Vallecito Mountains opposite the gypsum mine. There was no doubt about it. The gargantuan imprints in sandstone could only have been made those eons ago when the earth was still soft and prehistoric monsters roamed the hills. Some prints measured fourteen inches long by nine inches wide. Others, more circular, spread over a diameter of ten or twelve inches.

Then along came those pedantic doubting Thomases who carry titles like archaeologist, geologist, and paleontologist. " No," they said in their wisdom, "your dinosaur tracks are merely the result of erosive forces upon concretions in the sandstone. The sedimentary strata of this region falls in the Miocene or Pliocene eras, long after dinosaurs became extinct."

Which all meant: When the sandstone was yet soft, rocks and various other foreign matter became embedded in it and remained there during the long years it took the sandstone matrix to harden. Then finally, when the layer of sandstone became exposed to constant erosion by water and wind, the concretions, being harder and more resistant to weathering, were exposed in relief until loosened from their base. When they dropped out, they left the impressions we see today. Still, one has to wonder how random concretions could have assumed such remarkable uniformity in size and shape. It was more fun when they were dinosaur tracks.

HANK BRANDT'S LOST MINE IN
THE FISH CREEK MOUNTAINS

Hank Brandt was a French Canadian of German descent who worked a gold mine in Baja in the 1880s. Having amassed a considerable fortune, he was en route with it to the U.S. when he was attacked by Mexican bandits. A gunfight ensued. Hank managed to escape with his life, but not his gold. In the dark of night he worked his way across the border above Signal Mountain into the vicinity of Superstition Mountain. There, in some remote canyon, the lucky devil recouped his lost fortune with enough gold to keep him in luxury for the rest of his life.

When out on the desert working his mine, Brandt lived in a crude shack surrounded with a fence of human skulls he had found in the "malpais," Spanish for badlands. (One writer believed Brandt was the prankster responsible for skeletons old prospectors reportedly saw dancing around the badlands.)

Unlike some professed "gold finders," Brandt's wealth was verified. His shipments to the San Francisco Mint from Riverside are a matter of record. When he died in San Diego he left $16,000 in gold to the friend in whose home he died.

Brandt's class of gold departs from the black-coated placer nuggets usually reported in this area. His was free gold matrixed in rusty quartz veins or streamers gleaned from a one-man, hard-rock digging. Shortly before he died, having accumulated enough wealth to outlast his life, Brandt divulged a waybill to his mine. With desert areas still virtually unexplored in those days, it consisted of landmarks that varied with interpretation.

The waybill included a place where jade was found, several petrified palms, some whale bones, two dry lakes marked with two ironwood trees, a canyon with reddish-brown sandstone walls, the imprint of a petrified ship in sandstone, a wall of purple talc, a double-decked cave, another cave filled with *ollas*, a seepage around which a large swarm of bees continually buzzed, and a canyon filled with mesquite near a high bank out from which cropped a boulder with a huge ocotillo on top. The mine was in a hidden valley above that spot. Good luck!

Victor Stoyanow, a *Desert Magazine* writer whom we will meet in the Anza-Borrego chapter, might have been misled by his Abominable Sandman discovery. He was not misled in his dedication to locate the legendary Hank Brandt mine. After years of searching, he concluded that the initial error in the waybill was not deliberate prevarication on Brandt's part, but resulted from Brandt's limited knowledge of what he had actually seen. For instance, there is no jade in the area, but Stoyanow found a float of green rock. It was probably Amazonite (greenish microcline feldspar) or a pyroxene (perhaps jadeite), which to Brandt had resembled jade. Brandt's "whale" bones were in reality mastodon tusks, remains of prehistoric elephants that once roamed the area. Brandt's petrified palms were the stands of rock coveted by rock hounds today.

Charlie Knowles, a prospector who spent three years in a fruitless search for the Hank Brandt mine, made three positive postulations: the mine was within a five-mile radius of Fish Creek Mountains; it definitely existed as a source of high-yield gold; and it would be found by accident. He was right on all counts.

Arriving within a mile of Fish Creek Mountains, Stoyanow had uncovered every clue. And still, the mine eluded him. More intent upon a career as a writer than one as a prospector, he sent us a story outlining his conquest up to that point. He concluded his story with these words directed toward *Desert* readers: Next winter I'll strike out again—unless you come across it before then. If you do, drop me a line—after you file your claim—so I can close the case.

A few years later my mail included a letter from a reader named Myrtle Teague. "Close the door on Hank Brandt," she wrote. "We found it accidentally while searching for Pegleg's black nuggets."

Towing their 4-wheel drive behind a camper, the Teagues had set out for a week of exploring. They made camp in an area convenient to the canyons of Fish Creek Mountains, planning to start at the north end and work their way east. On the fifth day they headed around the eastern slope and drove as far as possible before continuing into a big canyon on foot.

Near its mouth was a dim trail which they followed into a narrow canyon framed on two sides by steep walls. High up on the left side yawned a double-decked cave. A devoted reader of *Desert Magazine*, Myrtle recognized it as a clue to the Hank Brandt mine. Excited, they hurried along the weak trail to a small mesa surrounded by reddish brown sandstone. Then they were really stopped. Carved of sandstone above their heads loomed a perfect replica of a ship—another Hank Brandt clue!

It was hot and they were tired, so they uncapped their canteens and paused for a rest. But they might as well have continued, for just around the next bend they came upon a thirty-foot deep hole surrounded by tailings—Hank Brandt's one-man digging.

Within a few feet of the mine stood a cairn with a claim notice in a tin can. Trembling with excitement, Myrtle drew out a paper

Painted Canyon, north fork beyond the dry waterfall in Mecca Hills.–JRL

inscribed with green ink. It read, "Hank's Lost Mine," and was dated 1951. Unsigned, the Teagues imagined that whoever had found it first had taken the gold and for reasons of his own, kept it secret.

While relating this incident, I was reminded of a retired London journalist who was interviewing an amateur Egyptologist whose hobby was searching for an old tomb in Egypt that was known to exist, but not where. After many futile years, the Egyptologist was among the party that finally uncovered it.

"How exciting that must have been!" the journalist exclaimed.

"It was not," growled the old man. "The excitement was when we *couldn't* find it."

There may be something to that, but the sheer adventure of finding the elusive mine was reward enough for the Teagues.

OLD TRUCKHAVEN TRAIL AND PALM WASH

Back to the Salton Sea and a short distance north of Salton City lies the turnoff to Borrego-Salton Seaway, S-22, known locally as the old Truckhaven Trail. This route began in 1929 when Doc Beaty, an early homesteader and promoter of Borrego Valley, conceived the idea of a wagon road passing between Borrego Badlands and Santa Rosa Mountains to facilitate travel between Borrego Valley and Coachella Valley.

Local merchants donated money, food, mules, equipment and labor, but hardly had the road been completed when storms

Travertine Rock.–LEL

gashed its grades and gutted its roadbeds. Until the area became a state park, maintenance was too expensive for the homesteaders to handle alone. Even after that, with bulldozers periodically clearing it, the trail was rarely used. But now, and since 1968 when it was paved, passenger car motorists can visit this extraordinary terrain where awesome views of delicately tinged badlands cascade into sandy, palm-strewn washes surrounded on all sides by miles of sun-varnished rocks, black as Pegleg's legendary gold.

If you look carefully to the north as you drive along the Old Truckhaven Trail, you will notice the frond of a palm tree thrust above Palm Wash to the north. It signals a favorite campground for rock hounds searching for petrified palm wood and concretion fantasies that are constantly weathering out of the sedimentary deposits of these clay hills. In 1936, Randall Henderson counted twenty-two mature Washingtonia palms and five young ones reported growing along the wash. There are fewer today.

TRAVERTINE ROCK AND PREHISTORIC FISHTRAPS

Travertine Rock looms up on the west side of Highway 86, opposite Desert Shores Resort. By turning off onto a paved segment of the old highway that parallels the present one, you can park your car and explore this intriguing area by foot.

A plaque, erected in 1968 by the Roads to Romance Association and the Coachella Valley Historical Association, used to tell the story before it was stolen. Now at elevation ninety-nine feet

below sea level, some five-hundred years ago, when ancient Lake
Cahuilla existed, the plaque would have been 139 feet underwater.
This accounts for the beach line so clearly visible along the base of
the Santa Rosa Mountains that frame the valley. Travertine Rock is
a granite outcrop covered by a hard crust of calcium carbonate deposited by receding waters of the ancient lake. Its chalk-like surface is marked with indelible pre-historic human handprints and
petroglyphs which, unfortunately have been almost obliterated by
the graffiti of modern ones.

Unique prehistoric "fishtraps" were constructed by unknown
dwellers in the Salton Trough when magical waters produced sudden inland seas. They may be seen on the east slope of the Santa
Rosas at the west end of Avenue 66, which intersects S-86 at Va-
lerie Jean. Their true purpose remains shrouded in mystery. The
circular depressions, four to twelve feet in diameter, may have
formed stone pens along the water's edge into which fish entered
and remained trapped when the tide lowered. They are best seen
in the long shadow hours of early morning or late afternoon from
a vantage point on the hillside at the ancient water line. Local inquiry is necessary to locate this site.

FIGTREE JOHN

Another legendary figure along this route was an old Cahuilla Indian named Juanita Razon, better known as Figtree John, who
once lived here in a mud-and-arrow hut shaded by fig trees. Customarily taciturn with strangers, whom he greeted with his trusty
Winchester rifle in hand, he was so enchanted with the blue uni-
forms of a lost detachment of soldiers who found their way to his
hut in the 1880s that he gave them food and water and guided them
back to their intended trail.

As a show of appreciation to their savior, the soldiers resolved
to send him a uniform. When it arrived, it came accompanied by a
formal stovepipe hat. The top hat may have seemed like a good
joke to the soldiers, but to old Figtree the uniform and formal hat
bolstered self-confidence when he conducted his entrepreneurial
dealings in the desert community. Dressed for the occasion, in
spite of bare feet, he swung a mighty bargain after the Colorado
River disgorged its waters into the Salton Sink. Commanding a
crew of workmen, Figtree salvaged railroad ties abandoned by the
Southern Pacific and the two salt companies which he then sold
for a nice profit.

In *Golden Mirages* Philip Bailey tells about an early railroad
surveyor who camped one night at Figtree John's spring when a

rider arrived to water his burro and fill his canteen. Joining the surveyor under John's ramada, the stranger volunteered that he had been living with Indians at Palma Seca well (Indian Well) on the old Yuma road where a squaw had informed him of a little black hill south of Travertine Point covered with gold when the wind blew just right. To prove his point, he showed the men a nugget as large as an acorn which the squaw had given to him. After a long silence, Figtree cryptically remarked, "Hills don't move, but the place where they are does." Bailey interpreted this as meaning that Figtree John knew of such a place, but not in that vicinity.

One more enigma to add to the "Pegleg Saga!"

NORTH AND EAST SHORE MOUNTAINS

During the month of March, the scenic North Shore route around Salton Sea is the best Coachella Valley area for taking photographs of desert wildflowers. Dominant species in bloom then are purple verbena, delicate evening primrose, and the bright, sweet-smelling desert sunflower. Some years are spectacular, others only so-so. Three conditions determine the display—well-spaced and adequate rainfall through winter and early spring, sufficient warmth of sun, and a lack of desiccating winds.

NILAND AND S-111

Niland, received its name as a result of a contest when the winner compared its fertile soil to that of the fabled Valley of the Nile. At the end of Noffsinger Street, which intersects S-111, dry ice wells bubble up along the shore. Unlike the submerged mud volcanoes at Mullet Island, these are cold to the touch.

MECCA

This settlement received its exotic name because it resembles the Arabian Mecca in climate, but it was first called Walters and consisted only of a siding on the Southern Pacific line to provide water from its 1,500-foot well. It was also a staging point for gold and silver mines in nearby mountains. The first experimental date gardens were planted here and remnants of the old Caravansary adobe hotel, the first in the area, still stand. Receiving water from the All American Canal, Mecca is now celebrated as the earliest producer of spring vegetables (January and February).

A few miles east of Mecca is Hidden Springs and Painted Canyon where Cahuilla Indians once camped.

HIDDEN SPRINGS—WASH NUMBER 31
ON CANAL ROAD

This Hidden Springs oasis once was famed as a secluded spot for lovers to enjoy discreet outings. Then photographers and rock hounds discovered its rich bounty of fossilized shells, quartz, bloodstone and vivid scenic splendor. It no longer provides a haven for lovers, but it is surely a place you want to visit if you have a 4-wheel drive. The All-American Canal blocked its entrance until a new approach was discovered via Wash Number 31 on the Canal Road. Canal numbers, incidentally, are for the purpose of marking locations where canal water is diverted beneath washes.

To reach the oasis, go north from S-111 on Vanderveer Road to Canal Road. Cross the canal at Wash Number 31 and proceed up the wash for two miles. Turn left over a rise that drops into another wash and follow it for three more miles. At that point the road winds around a large tree. Turn right there, continue along the wash for another three miles and this will bring you close to the entrance of Hidden Spring. The entrance is blasted out of solid black rock and is easily identified. Only practiced drivers should try this road in any other than a four-wheel drive vehicle.

PAINTED CANYON

Directly east of Mecca on S-195 and immediately after crossing the All-American Canal, a graded dirt road leads north to lovely Painted Canyon in the Mecca Hills. Cahuilla Indians once camped here and their potsherds are still scattered among fossilized shells, quartz and bloodstone specimens that bring picnicking rock hounds into the area. It starts out looking like mudhills as heavily carved by nature as a Bali temple and progresses into richly colored marble halls. Smoke trees in the washes lend softness to the stark red, pink and orange strata forming canyon walls. It is indeed a "painted canyon;" one overlooked even by locals. Coves along the trail that winds through the canyon provide countless camping spots.

A magnificent view of Salton Sea framed by the distant Santa Rosas spreads into the horizon as the road spins out of the Mecca Hills.

DOS PALMAS SPRING

A dirt offshoot from the All American Canal Road at the end of short Parkside Drive east from the Salton Sea Recreation Area Headquarters leads ultimately to Dos Palmas Spring. (See AAA map

"Riverside County") This was once an important water stop and is now a desert preserve. Lt. Romuldo Pacheco with Capt. Jose Romero stopped here while attempting to establish a route from San Bernardino to Yuma. Pacheco reported that the route was impracticable. Later, forty-niners trekking westward on their run to California gold fields decided the same thing. Most of them preferred the Yuma-San Diego route, or the variation via Warner's Ranch.

When gold was discovered at La Paz on the Colorado River in 1862 by Pauline Weaver, however, the trek began to take a turn in the opposite direction. As a result, William D. Bradshaw led a road-building party through San Gorgonio Pass to what is now Palm Springs and then on to Travertine Rock, from where they turned east into the sandy basin that was Salton Sink and crossed to Dos Palmas Spring and thence on to Chuckwalla Wells and the Colorado River. Using a map provided by Cocomaricopa Indian mail runners, with additional help from Cahuilla Indians who lived near Travertine Rock, Bradshaw established the famous route given his name. A stage line run by Alexander & Co. carried passengers along it, while Bradshaw handled the freight line. By 1863, other stages also used this route.

When the Southern Pacific Railroad finally reached across the Colorado at Yuma in September of 1877, use of the Bradshaw Road dwindled, but railroad workers and early residents used a regional stage line that still operated out of Dos Palmas. The spring also remained as a rallying point in 1885 when gold mines were operating in the Orocopias.

A crude stone marker near the old stage road reads, "Baby White, Borne December 1903," a grim indicator of the hardships of travel in those days.

Dos Palmas also figured in a lost treasure legend which involved a stagecoach hold-up. The driver was murdered and robbed of a cargo of gold before reaching the station, but the robber arrived at the bar to celebrate his success. When he paid for his booze with raw gold, it aroused suspicion. The sheriff was notified. By the time he discovered the crime and returned to the stage, the robber had become alerted to the fact that he was "wanted." In making his escape, he was shot and killed, but not before stashing the gold somewhere. It has never been found.

Frank Coffey, a colorful jackass prospector, made his home here after graduating from mining school in the 1880s. Coffey had been sent by an eastern syndicate to report on gold and silver property in the Chocolate Mountains. The area proved unpromising, but the romantic life of a single-blanket prospector appealed to him so he resigned his job, acquired a string of burros, pro-

Dos Palmas Spring.-*JRL*

claimed himself "Mayor of Dos Palmas" (pop. 1), and lived there until he died in 1936.

Although Coffey chose a lonely home on the isolated desert for himself, he was paradoxically a social being. It was he who, upon discovering the gravesite of the baby who had died on the pioneer trail, installed a proper marker for the unknown child he called "Poor Baby White." Other old-timers liked to recall that Coffey never left a camp when he was out prospecting without gathering wood for those who might come that way later.

SALTON SEA STATE RECREATION AREA

The Sea and Desert Interpretive Visitors Center, located on the east shore at State Park Road, presents a twenty-minute video show that covers the history of this thirty-five-mile-long, eighteen-mile-wide inland sea. It is open daily October through May.

MURDER OF HERMAN EHRENBERG

Another tragedy left its ghost at Dos Palmas when Herman Ehrenberg, founder of an early town that bore his name on the Arizona side of the Colorado, was killed there on the night of October 9, 1866. Speculations regarding his assailant tantalize historians even today.

Because a few items were missing from the store, blame initially fell on "an evilly disposed" Indian, until the proprietor of Dos Palmas House, one W. H. Smith, gave his version. Discounting

Indians altogether, Smith charged an unknown mining rival of Ehrenberg's from the Colorado River region for the murder. At the same time, other arrivals suspected that Smith himself was drunk and shot Ehrenberg by mistake.

The way it happened, Ehrenberg was on his way back to Arizona from a business trip to San Bernardino when his mule broke down and he was forced to quit the company of his companions. Shortly thereafter he joined some passing freighters that included Michael Goldwater and his son Morris, progenitors of the famous Arizonian Barry. Ehrenberg's mule recovered within a short distance of Dos Palmas so he left the slow-moving freighters and hurried on alone. At the oasis he bedded down on a pallet outside the door of Dos Palmas House. About midnight, Smith claimed to have heard a shot. First on the scene, he discovered his guest dying. By morning, the freighters had arrived and helped bury the body.

In a 1993 issue of *American Desert* magazine, other information was presented by writer Francis J. Johnson these 127 years after the fact. Charles Poston, an Arizona politician who had just lost an Arizona Territorial election, chose that seemly time to take a short leave from the territory. On the night of October 8, he slept at Dos Palmas House on the same pallet as Ehrenberg slept on the following night. For some reason, Poston had formed a deep distrust of Smith. After departing Dos Palmas, Poston had met Ehrenberg traveling in the opposite direction along the same route. During their short visit, Ehrenberg disclosed that he was carrying $3,500 in gold which he had borrowed on the coast to buy a mine. Poston charged that Smith had killed Ehrenberg to get the gold.

Then, to compound matters, a suspect named Hank Brown was introduced. This one, a raucous stage driver with a penchant for propositioning Indian maidens and beating up their escorts, had had an altercation the night previous to Ehrenberg's murder at Mule Springs while driving an old rancher named McCoy to Dos Palmas. Leaving early the next morning, Brown and his passenger arrived at the latter oasis the same night as Ehrenberg. At Dos Palmas House Brown habitually slept on a pallet beside the door, but on this night he gave the space to Ehrenberg. It was McCoy's belief that the Indian whom Brown affronted had tracked them from Mule Springs and murdered the sleeping man, believing he was Brown.

So here we are with four suspects for the murder of Ehrenberg at Dos Palmas in 1866: W. H. Smith, proprietor of Dos Palmas, an Indian seeking revenge on Hank Brown, an Indian trying to rob the store, and possibly a business rival from Arizona. Take your pick.

When automobiles began to travel through this area, ranchers and miners packed the rutted roads with straw in order to keep cars from getting stuck in sand. It also made easier going for horses pulling wagons, until an occasional careless driver dropped a lighted cigarette and burned up the road.

HOT MINERAL SPA ROAD

Fountain of Youth Spa and Bashford's Hot Mineral Spa both lie on this road, which is east of Bombay Beach. They are therapeutic natural wonders with mineral waters bubbling from the ground at 170 degrees. These are the only hot springs in the nation with the same rock and mineral properties found in the springs of Yellowstone National Park.

SALTON SEA NATIONAL WILDLIFE REFUGE

With the dry, almost barren desert on the one side and rich agricultural crops on the other, this below-sea-level refuge is one of the most interesting in the entire National Wildlife Refuge system. It is reached via Sinclair Road from Hwy 111, halfway between Niland and Calipatria. Birds migrating here regularly are the Canadian snow goose, doves, gull-billed terns, laughing gulls, white-faced ibises, fulvous tree ducks, pelicans and flocks of shore birds including the amusing roadrunner, Gambel's quail and the cactus wren.

Camping and picnicking are not permitted on the refuge, but tours through the main waterfowl concentration areas may be arranged through the refuge manager. Portions of the refuge are opened during some years to waterfowl hunting in accordance with existing federal and state laws. Permits are handled by the California Department of Fish and Game at refuge headquarters.

OBSIDIAN BUTTE

West on Sinclair Street from Highway-111, Obsidian Butte rises from the shore of the Salton Sea. The black glass mound is only one of the oddities along this part of the lake. Years ago, bubbling mud pots were the main attraction, but they are now covered with water. A row of power poles protruding above water marks a submerged road that once connected what is now an island to the mainland. Along the shore may be found pumice, another form of volcanic glass.

In this area, also, a geothermal well was brought in on New Year's Day, 1964. The objective for it, and for others drilled since, is to explore the potential of incipient steam geysers to generate

Salton Sea National Wildlife Refuge, *southeast near Obsidian Butte.–LEL*

electricity necessary for desalinization of Salton Sea and water from the Gulf of California. If successful, this would ultimately augment water from the Colorado River for irrigating Imperial Valley and Mexico. According to scientists, Imperial Valley has one of the largest geothermal potentials in the world, a promising energy alternative that would save millions of barrels of oil each year. The U.S. Bureau of Reclamation, jointly with the University of California at Riverside, has inaugurated an ambitious experiment to determine exactly what that possibility is. Presently, the world's largest geothermal wellhead assembly is operated by the Cooper Oil Tool Division which controls steam production that generates enough electrical power for a town of thirty thousand persons for one year.

CHOCOLATE MOUNTAINS

To the east of Niland are the aptly named Chocolate Mountains, rich with old mines, historic trails and potential archaeological sites. Unfortunately they are closed to the public and have been since World War II. The military maintains them as an aerial gunnery range, with no encouragement that they will be released to public domain in the foreseeable future. If ever the range is opened to the public, it will be the last large desert "frontier" in southern California still unexplored by backcountry vehicles.

CALIPATRIA

Billed as the "lowest-down city in the Western Hemisphere" because it lies 184 feet below sea level, Calipatria is famous for its standard that floats a flag at the exact level of the Pacific Ocean.

NEW RIVER AND ALAMO RIVER

Highway-111 crosses New River and a short distance further, Alamo River. During the flood years of 1905-6 these two rivers flowed as one to turn the empty Salton Sink into a sea. Along their banks, stumpy palm trees grow so bountifully their bushy fronds resemble Queen Elizabeth's skirts. Farms raising crops and cattle spread in all directions, remindful of the happy fact that Imperial Valley produces more beef-pounds than any other single area in the world and that at certain times of the year, ninety percent of all vegetables eaten at tables in the U.S. come from this rich soil.

An intriguing story in a 1906 *San Diego News* item tells of one Thomas Moore coming upon a cache of gold weighing between fifty and sixty pounds in the sandy bank of the Alamo river. The twenty-pound ingots apparently had been buried years earlier and exposed to view by the crumbling riverbank. Mr. Moore cashed in his find for some $10,000. No one knew how they happened to be buried there, but it was assumed that the original carrier had been escaping robbers or unfriendly Indians and had hastily buried the cache to lighten his load.

ROADRUNNERS

Anywhere on the outskirts of desert communities—sometimes in residential areas—you are liable to see a skinny long-tailed bird dash across your path. This is the roadrunner, every desert lover's favorite clown. A member of the cuckoo family, *Geococcyx californianus*, the bird will stand up to a rattlesnake. They also have been known to feast on lizards, rats, mice, ground squirrels and they aren't above robbing other bird's eggs. They build their nests close to the ground and do more running than flying.

Anza-Borrego Desert

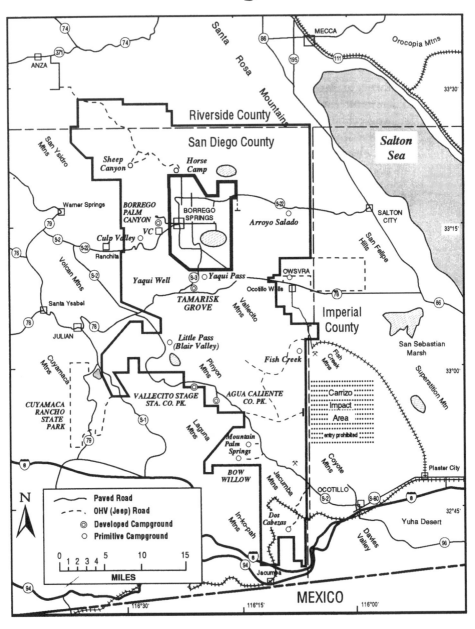

CHAPTER 3

ANZA-BORREGO DESERT

THE ANZA ROUTE

Old trails, haunting legends, emeralds, quirky characters, the Mormon Battalion trek and ghost tales comprise only a mere part of Anza-Borrego's fascination.

Jesuit missions had been established in Baja California and in northern Sonora and Franciscan friars were colonizing Alta California along the Pacific coast. The time now was due to link the mission system by land. In 1771, the indefatigable Francisco Garces came from Mission San Xavier de Bac near Tucson to wend a confused path as far west of the big river as Calexico, but it was not until a later trip, as spiritual advisor to Captain Juan Bautista de Anza's Colorado Desert expedition to the California missions in 1774, that Garces was launched upon a traceable route.

Then, in 1775, Anza made a second journey, this time bringing 240 persons and a thousand head of cattle. It was mid-winter, intensely cold, and water and forage was scarce. The fevered animals broke away in search of it, and the party divided so as not to arrive at water holes at the same time. These early day emigrants went on to establish the pueblo of San Francisco. Hardships they endured are legend today, but their tracks over the hard rocky land interspersed with shifting dunes and through formidable mountain passes establishing this Spanish land route to California. Later, a more southern route (today's S-2) would be discovered and followed by trappers, explorers, gold seekers and troops of General Stephen W. Kearney's United States Army of the West.

BORREGO SPRINGS

This popular retirement community, the focus point for Anza-Borrego Desert State Park, was founded by cattlemen who began homesteading about 1875. Farmers followed when a well bringing up good water was discovered in 1926 and a post office was established.

After World War II, developers subdivided the area and the present resort community with posh golf courses arose. Although land within city limits is privately owned, it is entirely surrounded by the park. Borrego Springs appeals especially to second-homeowners who desire a less glitzy environment than the Palm Springs area offers. Numerous accommodations, eating establishments and shops cater to a winter colony of "snow birds."

ANZA-BORREGO DESERT STATE PARK

Anza-Borrego Desert State Park is divided into two parts. The northern (Borrego) sector was established in 1933, the southern (Anza) sector added in 1957. The park is administered by the California Department of Parks and Recreation and supervised by state park rangers. Therefore, wildlife is protected, no removal of vegetation is permitted, archaeological relics must be left undisturbed, vehicles must remain on approved routes of travel and commercial activities are prohibited. A majority of the roads are unpaved. Convenient campgrounds are located throughout the park as well as marked hiking trails. Further information may be obtained at ranger stations or at park headquarters in Borrego Springs.

The unusual visitor's center on Palm Canyon Drive is a masterful example of desert architecture. Built partly underground, it not only blends beautifully with its environment but is also solar oriented, economizing on energy. The Visitor Center is open weekdays from October through May and every weekend all year round. Fifteen-minute slide shows present a fine overview of the park's seasonal flora, the bighorn sheep, and the desert in all seasons. Other exhibits focus on desert geology, fauna, flora and history.

It would require a lifetime to explore the vast area of the park in its entirety. Because our emphasis in this book is upon mysteries, legends, and tales of the southern California desert, we recommend that those who wish to follow Anza-Borrego's countless four-wheel-drive and hiking trails refer to one of the excellent guidebooks devoted exclusively to this area that are available at the visitor center's bookshop. We particularly recommend *Anza-Borrego Desert Region* by Lowell and Diana Lindsay.

IMPERIAL HIGHWAY S-2

Crossing the park from southeast to northwest, the Imperial Highway (S-2) follows a route opened during the Mexican period (1821-1847). Except for a short time when threatened by Indian uprisings, it was the principal artery of early travel through this desert region to the west coast via Warners Ranch. At various times the trail has been called the Sonora Road, the Colorado Road, the Emigrant Trail, and the Butterfield Overland Mail Route.

It was the also the trail followed by the Mormon Battalion.

MORMON BATTALION

Forced to leave Missouri and Illinois and refused admission to Arkansas, the Church of Jesus Christ of Latter-day Saints (Mormon) decided to move to the far West. In January of 1846 Brigham Young dispatched an agent to Washington with instructions to take advantage of any facilities the United States Government might offer the Saints to migrate to the Pacific coast. As luck would have it, the agent arrived in May about a week after the outbreak of the Mexican War. Since President Polk was determined to take possession of California and in need of men for the military expedition, Polk had no trouble winning the cabinet's unanimous decision to enlist Mormon volunteers in order "to conciliate them, attach them to our country, and prevent them from taking part against us."

Thus the call to arms: "An opportunity is now available to the Mormon people to send a portion of their young and intelligent men to the ultimate destination of their whole people entirely at the expense of the United States; and this advance party can pave the way, and look out the land for their brethren to come after them."

There was no difficulty in obtaining volunteers. Lt. Colonel Philip St. George Cooke was appointed commander of the Mormon Battalion with orders to open a wagon road to the Pacific. After crossing the Colorado a few miles below Yuma and learning that the first well in the sandy terrain ahead was fifteen miles distant, Cooke pushed his bedraggled legion onward, their mules restless and the tar on the wagon wheels stiff with cold. Some of the supply wagons, sheep, mules, and cattle had been left behind at the river with hope that Cooke could send for them when the battalion needed fresh supplies.

One particularly poignant incident occurred when Pauline Weaver, the troop's trapper-guide, had led them in a desperate need of water to an abandoned Indian well. Unfortunately it was in quicksand and kept caving in. After every possible expedient to open it had failed, they concluded that the only hope was in using a washtub that belonged to a captain and his wife. Unbelievably, since all of their lives depended on it, the couple refused to give up this valuable article! Cooke, of course, took it anyway.

His trail followed closely below the present Mexican border until it led them northward to a well known as Alamo Mocho, then continued in a northwesterly direction to Pozo Hondo, a short distance west of El Centro. From there the route to Warner's Ranch, where they hoped to rendezvous with General Stephen W. Kearney's expedition, led to Carrizo Creek in the present Anza-Borrego Desert State Park.

CARRIZO CREEK AND THE PHANTOM STAGE

The march to Carrizo Creek proved longer and harder for the Mormons than was expected. Their day started with fifty-seven mules; it ended with only twenty-two. Besides being nearly starved, the mules had been without water for three days. Ten miles of dreaded sand still lay before them. You can imagine with what joy Cooke finally wrote in his journal, "A clear, running stream gladdened our eyes after the anxious dependence upon muddy wells for five or six days" when they reached Carrizo Creek.

A mainstay of diet during the long arid march was the mesquite bean which the brethren ate raw or ground and mixed in flour for bread or pudding, but even that grew scarce.

Of their march through the Anza-Borrego Desert, Corporal Tyler of the Mormon Battalion wrote in his journal, "We found here

Carrizo Gorge. *Railroad tracks on mountainside, 1977. Photo courtesy of California Department of Parks and Recreation.*

Palm Wash. *SD&AE tracks washed out by Hurricane Kathleen, 1976.–LEL*

the heaviest sand, hottest days, and coldest nights with no water
and but little food. At this time many of the men were nearly bare-
foot with rawhide or cast-off clothing wrapped about their feet. Before we arrived at the Carrizo, many were so used up from thirst,
hunger and fatigue that they were unable to speak until water was
brought to them. Others had been left lying exhausted by the
way-side."

The old Carrizo Stage Station that lies at the end of the Carrizo
Creek road was on the Southern Overland stage route of 1849 that
passed along the Carrizo Corridor. Therein lies one of the desert's
eerie ghost stories.

Philip Bailey, a desert writer who recounted the legend in his
book *Golden Mirages*, had heard so many desert rats testify to a
phantom four-mule stagecoach with a lone driver that rumbled
along the old trail on moonless nights that he did some research.
What he learned was that a stage had disappeared near Carrizo
back in the 1860s. It had started out with a driver, a guard, and a
box of gold bound for San Diego, but when the guard became ill,
the driver left him and continued on alone into the desert. At Carrizo Wash, bandits held up the stage, stole the gold, and shot the
driver dead, leaving him slumped over the reins with the team
racing onward to a destination it will never reach. Ever since,
the stage has returned to haunt Carrizo Wash. More than a few

old-time desert rats claimed that the phantom coach left wheel ruts in the soft soil.

LEGEND OF THE VIKING SHIP

Legends of ancient vessels foundering in this area's countless transitions from sandpit to sea are as rampant as Pegleg's black gold. If legend is based upon fact, as many of us believe, then *all* of those sightings can't be ignored.

One persistent story concerns Señora Petra Tucker who, before she married her prospecting husband, was the widow of one Santiago Socia. It was Santiago who first found an "ancient ship of the desert." He had recently moved from Mexico City to Tecate where Petra was to join him. While awaiting her, he met a peon who had a waybill to several *ollas* filled with gold buried in the United States desert about forty kilometers northeast of Tecate. Armed with the map, which he had purchased from the peon, he set forth immediately after Petra's arrival.

A month later Santiago returned to Petra, poorer but wiser, although not empty-handed. The souvenir he brought home was a shield made of metal in the shape of a tortilla, only larger.

Santiago had a strange story to tell. While searching for the treasure, he had entered several canyons near the floor of the desert. In the bottom of one with high sheer walls stood an ancient ship with round discs on its side. Only a portion of the ship projected from the sand. There was strange writing on the wall above the ship which Santiago didn't recognize as Indian, Spanish or English. The bow of the ship was curved and carved like the long neck of a bird. It was one of the discs attached to the ship's side that he had brought home to Petra. When she remarried after Santiago's death, it was discarded, but she often spoke of the strange ship.

An intriguing record turned up in Guadalajara, Mexico, in the mid-'50s that revealed an official inquiry held by the Spanish court in 1574. A strange fleet of three large and five small vessels had been sighted sailing north in the Gulf of California. The vessels resembled Galician caravels with carved pelican figureheads. Because they obviously were not of Spanish origin, the Crown had ordered an investigation. Witnesses included Spanish soldiers and Indians who lived in pueblos along the western coast of Mexico. All described the vessels in a similar manner. One of the witnesses was a Franciscan friar who was brought up in a European seaport and was familiar with the sailing vessels of many nations. Never had he seen vessels such as these.

No conclusion was reached, nor is there any mention of a vessel of this description being seen again—until 1933, a year remembered in southern California because of the great earthquake which leveled the city of Long Beach and caused damage for many miles around.

Myrtle and Louis Botts of Julian often came down from their mountain home to camp on the desert. Their favorite spot was near what now is the established Agua Caliente County Park, but hardly anyone knew of it in the '30s when the Botts camped here.

While Myrtle prepared a Dutch oven dinner one evening, a dusty old prospector arrived to replenish his water supply. A few days earlier, he told the Botts, he had been far into a canyon where he had seen an old ship sticking right out of the side of a mountain. Because he also claimed to know where the Pegleg gold was, the Botts laughed and went on with their dinner.

Myrtle was a serious amateur botanist, one of the founders of the famous wildflower show held annually in Julian. It was to survey the rain situation and to search for possible new specimens that she and her husband had come to this remote area. The following day they pursued their quest with eyes fastened to the ground as they hiked along the floor of a previously unlisted defile. When the grade grew steeper, they paused to rest. Myrtle noticed it first.

Jutting out of the canyon wall, almost immediately overhead, was the forward portion of a large and very ancient vessel. A curved stem head swept up from its prowl. Along both sides of the vessel were clearly discernible circular marks in the wood, quite possibly left by shields which at one time had been attached to the

Lake Cahuilla. The water line of the ancient lake shown here suggests the possibility of one or more ships entrapped in the Salton Basin after entry via the Colorado River.–CP

vessel. Near the bow, on one side of the ship, were four deep fur-
rows in the wood. The craft was high enough to hide its interior
from their view and the side of the canyon so precipitous and unstable, being composed of shale and clay, that they doubted it
would support much weight. The Botts studied the curious sight
for a long time before carefully retracing their steps to camp so as
to be able to relocate it.

Hardly had they emerged from the canyon when the earthquake struck. Both were thrown to the ground as they watched
their camp being shaken to pieces. When the rumble subsided, the
Botts recovered their scattered supplies and hurried home, but not
before discovering that the spring which had been cold the night
before was now hot.

I interviewed Myrtle Botts before relating her experience in
The Mysterious West, a book I wrote in 1967 with Brad Williams.
She was the librarian in charge of the Julian Public Library, which
gave her access to a wealth of research material to help identify
the ship she had seen. Preliminary investigation suggested an old
Viking ship, yet she found it hard to believe that the craft could be
one of those ancient piratical vessels. Before reporting her discovery, she wanted to confirm it with photographs. Thus the Botts returned the following weekend to Agua Caliente Springs.

Once again they hiked up the steep canyon, but this time when
they reached the spot where they had rested, the passage was
blocked. Half of the unstable mountainside had fallen into the
canyon during the earthquake. It was an uncomfortable feeling to
realize that had they remained there much longer, they would have
been buried under those tons of toppled earth.

Myrtle Botts, since deceased, struck me during our interview
as a sensible, down-to-earth woman not given to fanciful illusions.
In my experience, legend usually has a basis in fact. Her suggestion
of a Viking ship struck a familiar chord in my memory. During research for an article on Tiburon Island in the Gulf of Mexico, I had
run across a Seri Indian song that could be pertinent.

This once hostile and murderous tribe preserves its history
through song, a curious lilting monotone that is passed down
through generations by tribal historians trained for their task from
childhood. One song recounts the arrival of the "Came From Afar
Man." According to Seri legend, many, many years in the past there
appeared at Tiburon Island a huge boat that contained many large
men with yellow hair and a woman who wore her red hair braided
down her back. They remained at the island for many, many days
while the men went hunting with their arrows and spears. One
man, who was their chief, remained behind and lay with the

red-haired woman on the boat. When the hunters returned with their game, the boat departed from the land of the Series.

It is known that ancient Viking sea captains customarily carried their wives when they went to sea. Freydis, daughter of Eric the Red, was actually in command of a ship that sailed to the east coast of North America. It is known as well that other Vikings sailed to North America long before the Spanish. This could have been at a time when ancient Lake Cahuilla filled the Salton Sink to or above sea level with the Colorado River providing a waterway link to the sea.

Someday, perhaps, another earthquake will reopen the earth and again reveal the ancient vessel seen by the Botts. Their Agua Caliente location is indeed in the very active Elsinore Fault zone.

VALLECITO STAGE STATION AND THE LADY IN WHITE

This stage station lies along the Imperial Highway, but just outside the boundary of the Anza-Borrego Desert State Park. Between 1857 and 1861, it was the most famed way station along the Southern Emigrant Trail into California. The abundant water and green cienegas of Vallecito, which means "little valley" in Spanish, were a welcome sight after stage passengers' torturous days

Vallecito Stage Station, shown here restored.–LEL

of desert glare and heat, as it still is for picnickers and campers today.

During the Gold Rush, which began two years after Cooke's march, the public demanded a fast stage line along the southern route. In 1857 a contract was awarded to James E. Birch and the San Antonio and San Diego Mail Line was established, the first official transcontinental overland mail line in the United States. Coaches ran semi-monthly, instead of daily, between the two cities for the next fourteen months. But they did run on time, pulled by a six-mule hitch. Soon everyone was calling it the "Jackass Mail."

Service wasn't satisfactory however, so John Butterfield bought out the company and started service semi-weekly. He also extended the route by bypassing the port of San Diego and going to San Francisco via Los Angeles. There were 160 relay stations about eighteen miles apart along the 2,765-mile route from Tipton, Missouri. The trip was made in twenty-five days or less. One of the most important stops for both stage lines was the Vallecito Stage Station.

The original Butterfield Stage Station grew from a sod-brick house constructed for military use at Vallecito, unique because the sod-bricks were cut from the cienega rather than the usual adobe-brick. The roof construction was of hand-hewn beams

Vallecito Cemetary. *Legendary burial place of the "Lady in White."*
Photo by Hal Fisher, 4/1/90.

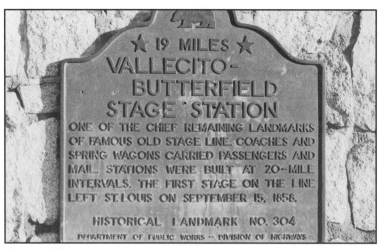

★ 19 MILES ★
VALLECITO-
BUTTERFIELD
STAGE STATION
ONE OF THE CHIEF REMAINING LANDMARKS
OF FAMOUS OLD STAGE LINE. COACHES AND
SPRING WAGONS CARRIED PASSENGERS AND
MAIL. STATIONS WERE BUILT AT 20-MILE
INTERVALS. THE FIRST STAGE ON THE LINE
LEFT ST. LOUIS ON SEPTEMBER 15, 1858.

HISTORICAL LANDMARK NO. 304
DEPARTMENT OF PUBLIC WORKS — DIVISION OF HIGHWAYS

Scissors Crossing. *Plaque at intersection of Hwys 78 and S-2, 19 miles northwest of the stage station.–LEL*

pegged and tied in place with rawhide, then a layer of willow poles followed by tules laid at right angles and topped with a coating of sod. After the stage line was discontinued, the sod building became a hideout for a Mexican bandit who, according to legend, deposited two gold-filled ollas (clay water jars) in a nearby canyon. The building you see now is a reconstructed model of the old station.

Any area that has witnessed so many tragic and violent events as these old desert trails have seen is bound to nourish a stock of ghost stories to keep the campfires burning. Carrizo Wash has its phantom stagecoach; Vallecito its "Lady in White."

This young lady was an Easterner en route to Sacramento to marry her fiancé who was making a fortune in the gold fields. The long, hard journey to reach the desert had tested her stamina, but crossing it in torrid heat left her totally depleted. At Vallecito Station she was taken from the stage deathly ill; and there she was buried in the bridal gown found in her luggage.

Countless witnesses claim that she lurks there yet. Should you choose to camp here on a dark night, you may still see the Lady in White wearily pacing the hard adobe ground as she awaits a stage to carry her to her lover. Scotty Macpherson, a volunteer park attendant, has seen her, and lots more apparitions.

ORIFLAMME MOUNTAIN AND GHOST LIGHTS

Just in case you missed a rendezvous with the Lady in White, don't give up. Anza-Borrego nourishes a hive of mysterious happenings. On some dark nights, about four miles west of Butterfield Ranch on the Imperial Highway, "ghost lights" may be dancing across the slopes of the fittingly named Oriflamme (golden flame) Mountain. Seen in other parts of the park as well, these "burning balls" that light up the sky have been reported since the 1880s. One occurrence of "spirit lights" was even investigated by the American Society for Psychical Research.

During the Prohibition era, it was suspected the lights were signal flares from bootleggers, but the glowing balls long outlived moonshiner's stills. Another theory popular with superstitious miners, before the park became a protected area, was that the mysterious lights, like the end of a rainbow, marked veins laden with gold. This idea gained credence from reports of legendary South American luminous balls that are believed to indicate buried treasure there.

Because the strange lights have been witnessed by too many sober judges to be ridiculed, scientists have searched for an explanation. One such explanation is that the lights result when dry desert winds blow sand against quartz outcroppings on the mountain to produce static electricity that flashes brightly against dark slopes.

That is the best they have come up with. A contender for the worst is that a coven of angry ghosts, Indians slaughtered by Spaniards are maintaining their ceaseless watch over a hidden cache of gold. Well, if those quartz outcroppings indicate gold, which they sometimes do, the "worst" might not be too far off base.

Russ Leadabrand was one who thought so. In a 1954 *Desert Magazine* story he recounted the plight of Harry Yarnell, a man who went into the Oriflamme Mountains in 1914, and actually saw that Indian gold.

Yarnell was a young farm hand hired to herd dairy stock from a ranch in Valley Center down to Imperial Valley where the feed was better. Accompanying him was a Mission Indian helper who called himself Julian Cabrias. Around the campfire at night Yarnell bragged of imagined adventures to Cabrias, while the Indian countered with stories of gold. When Yarnell challenged one of his tales, Cabrias said, "I will show you."

A few days later they arrived at Earthquake Valley in the Oriflammes. The stock was restless that evening so Cabrias went out to quiet them. When he returned to camp just after sunset, he held out his palm. "Look," he said to Yarnell, "I found these like I tell you." Firelight glittered on half a dozen golden nuggets, each the size of a peanut.

It was about a half-hour walk from their camp to the mouth of the small draw where Cabrias had picked up the gold. He often had heard his people tell of this place, he confided, and knew that great quantities of gold lay mixed in sand further up the gully.

Yarnell left a small cairn at the draw's mouth and promised himself that he would return as soon as his riding job was finished. But, true to the nature of lost gold yarns, upon arriving at El Centro he was offered a job too good to refuse. When he finally returned to the Oriflammes a year later, his cairn was gone.

Spring rains could have carried it away, or another prospector could have kicked it down. Yarnell prowled the canyon for a week trying to recognize the gully. Into some of them he crawled on his hands and knees, sifting sand through his fingers. Nothing appeared to be as he remembered it that night in the dim dusk. Nor could Yarnell locate Julian Cabrias again. Yet, he knew the gold was there. He had seen it with his own eyes.

Years passed. He never gave up. When Leadabrand met him, Yarnell was an old man, still prospecting in the Oriflammes.

Box Canyon. *Dry waterfall which forced the Mormon Battalion and other pioneers to build the difficult route at upper left of photo.–CP*

Gold was taken out of there in later years. A matter of record is a boulder of rock with wire gold sticking out of it that weighed a ton, found by George Benton, another prospector. Yarnell's golden gully, however, remains unfound.

BOX CANYON VIEWPOINT

The Mormon Battalion, crossing this desert range on one of the longest infantry marches in history, left behind a permanent memorial to resourcefulness. When the battalion stood at the entrance to Box Canyon, they had with them several large wagons that they had collected along the trail in the wake of Kearney's Army of the West. Kearney had been forced to abandon them in his rush to get to San Diego. As the soldiers advanced slowly into the canyon, they soon found themselves hemmed in by a vertical wall of granite fifteen feet high. Undaunted, they produced picks, axes, and crowbars to hammer the canyon walls until they had opened a passage wide enough to allow the wagons to pass through.

When the troops finally reached San Diego on January 29, 1847, they had traveled more than two thousand miles. Indeed, the Saints and their commander had reason to be proud. They had opened the first wagon road through the Southwest to California, used by thousands of emigrants who followed, and later established as a scheduled freight and passenger route.

An overlook here provides a view of the canyon and remnants of the road used by goldseekers, immigrants and Butterfield Overland Mail stagecoaches en route to Northern California. By climbing down rock steps along a footpath you can better appreciate the

Ghost Mountain. *Historic view of Marshal South's house approximately 1948. Photo courtesy of California Department of Parks and Recreation.*

Ghost Mountain. *Marshal South's house in 1976.–DEL*

awesome feat accomplished by those early Mormons who broke the trail.

GHOST MOUNTAIN AND THE MARSHAL SOUTH FAMILY

In the southeast corner of Blair Valley, a steep one-mile climb reveals the remains of Yaquitepec. This is an adobe house homesteaded in the 1930s by Marshal South, who with his poet wife Tanya and their three children, lived there "off the land." Thirty years later they would have been called "hippies," but in their time it may have been less a revolt against the establishment than a consequence of economic depression. Shoeless, and by choice without clothes, the family ground their own meal, depended for water upon rain caught in stone cisterns, made adobe from mud for shelter, modeled their own pottery, brewed squaw tea from desert herbs, toasted tortillas on the lid of an old coal-oil can, and lived as creatively as possible upon the meager sums Marshal earned from writing of their "experiment" in *Desert Magazine.*

The Souths gained quite a following during those Depression years. When asked why he had chosen to run out on civilization, South responded, "I did it to break the mold."

"A mold," he went on to say, "is a terrible thing, whether it be human thought or melted iron. The moment you pour it into a mold, you kill its individuality. It produces nothing but soulless, uninteresting mediocrity. In the case of my 'desert experiment,' I have broken the mold for myself, absolutely; for my children, almost definitely. In later years they may elect to associate with civilization, but it will have no power over their free thought. Truth will mean everything."

The South's writings in *Desert Magazine* appeared before I had purchased the publication, but in later years, I was curious to learn how the "experiment," which lasted about ten years, had ended. What I learned was rather disenchanting. Tanya was then living in San Diego following a bitter divorce from Marshal who had abandoned the marital "mold" in favor of a lady of "civilized" propensities. Tanya laughed at the "experiment" terminology, defining it more as "an escape from responsibility." The children were then grown, having adapted successfully to civilization.

SCISSORS CROSSING AND THE SAN FELIPE STAGE STATION

Here, where the intersection of Scissors Crossing rips through an old Indian cemetery, ghosts must be unhappy since the Indians revered their dead. Just behind the Vallecito Station historical marker at Scissors Crossing, 18 miles northwest of the actual station, the overland mail conductor would start blowing his coach horn to warn the San Felipe Station a mile distant that the stage was arriving for a quick change of horses or mules. The horn blast enabled employees to follow John Butterfield's instructions to his drivers that, "Nothing on God's earth must stop the United States Mail!"

BORREGO SINK AND THE ABOMINABLE SANDMAN

Moving now to the east of Borrego Springs, we come to the low point of Borrego Valley which receives the runoff from Coyote

Borrego Palm Canyon, 1972, north-west of Borrego Springs. Photo courtesy of Copley Books.

Canyon. Vegetation on its flanks is typical of desert growth in alkaline soil—mesquite, arroweed, desert thorn and bunch grass.
Back in 1939 it gave birth to a legend.

On a dark night while camping alone, a prospector was confronted by a pack of gigantic silver-haired beasts with red eyes that
glowed in the dark. Although they menaced him for some time,
they appeared to fear his blazing fire and kept a distance. No one
took the prospector's story very seriously until some thirty years
later Harold Lancaster, a well-respected desert wanderer, confirmed that some kind of strange beast was roaming the desert.
While camped in that same area, he was startled to see a "giant
apeman" approaching. Lancaster grabbed his shotgun and fired a
warning shot. The apeman "jumped a good three feet off the
ground," then high-tailed it back into the early morning shadows.

Although I personally pride myself on believing a little bit in
everything, I tend toward skepticism when it comes to a Sasquatch
of the desert, as evidenced by the following.

A manuscript written by Victor Stoyanow, a retired marine
major, passed across my desk at *Desert Magazine* in January 1964.
I had met the writer. In fact, I had suggested that he try his hand at
writing when he had dropped into the office to compare notes on
desert explorations. At every opportunity Stoyanow sought adventure in the most out-of-the way areas he could find. As it turned
out, he wrote very well and we published several of his stories.
And then came the one about the "Abominable Sandman!"

Our marine major had been tramping around one of the more
remote canyons in the Borrego Sink when he came across some in-
congruous tracks. Splay-toed and immense with clearly definable
digits terminating in tiny depressions made by claws, they pointed
downhill, each pair falling at an interval of approximately forty
inches. Upon reaching the desert floor, the tracks disappeared into
wind-blown sand. Continuing his search, the major found identical
prints on a nearby hill among some bunch grass where the ground
was softer. These tracks were about seven feet apart and slightly
larger than the others. From this, the major deduced that the monster was capable of prodigious leaps.

Returning to his home in San Diego, the major went through
San Diego Union files at the library. He found no reference to a
desert bigfoot, but he did learn that some years earlier a monster
had been killed by a Frank Cox at Deadman's Hole near Warner
Hot Springs on the northern fringe of the park. This monster was
described as having feet twenty-four inches long, weighing about
four hundred pounds and with a small head and buckteeth. It appeared to be a cross between a man and a bear. Satisfied with his

research, the major neglected to read a subsequent edition of the newspaper which revealed that the story had been published as an April Fool's joke.

The following weekend the major returned to Borrego. The tracks were still there so he made some plaster casts, took photos and wrote his story about the discovery. Within a few days after it was published, Borrego Valley was swarming with explorers seeking the Abominable Sandman, a foray which caused considerable frustration to rangers in the park who for months afterward were pulling sandman hunters out of deep sand.

Naturally I had to make a personal inspection of the phenomenon. Equipped with plaster-of-Paris to make our own cast and accompanied by members of the magazine staff, I was astonished to see a steer happily grazing down in the sink. Then, a short distance further we came upon some pads of dried dung. We kicked away one of the pads and took a cast of the impression it had left in the sand. It was virtually identical to the cast made by the enterprising major.

So much for the Abominable Sandman!

PEGLEG SMITH MONUMENT

Now an Anza-Borrego landmark, this haphazard pile of rocks bears a sign reading "Let him who seeks Pegleg Smith's gold add ten rocks to this monument." It may not be impressive, as monu-

Pegleg Smith Monument.–CP

ments go, but it is dear to the hundreds of pegophiles who have been attending the Liars' Contest held here annually on the first Saturday of each April. The site has no significance as to where Pegleg found his gold although it does lie within the perimeter set by the modern Mr. Pegleg.

The founding of the annual Pegleg Smith Liar's Contest actually has its beginnings in 1916 when Harry Oliver helped to start the Pegleg Smith Club composed of local residents from Borrego Valley who enjoyed telling tall tales. Oliver enjoyed perpetuating Pegleg's story and billed himself as "press agent for Pegleg's

Pegleg Smith Monument. *John Hilton, famous desert artist, was one of the organizers of the first Pegleg tall-tale ceremony on January 1, 1948. Photo courtesy of California Department of Parks and Recreation.*

ghost." He startled many an unsuspecting prospector who found one of the numerous peglegs Harry had whittled and hidden in isolated areas around the desert in the 1920s. Authors Philip Bailey and Erle Stanley Gardner both later wrote of a prospector who imagined himself hot on the "black gold" trail after finding an old, weathered pegleg. One had to wonder....

Oliver was also instrumental in beginning the first Lost Pegleg Mine Trek and in building the Pegleg Smith Monument. On January 1, 1948, Oliver and Ray Hetherington of Knott's Berry Farm invited desert *aficionados* to come and tell tall tales. Among the guests were the yet-to-become famous desert artist John Hilton, self-styled desert rat Steve Ragsdale, Desert Magazine founder Randall Henderson, and "Doc" A.A. Beaty who later launched the old Truckhaven Trail. Over 200 people attended that first trek with each placing the required ten rocks to the newly formed monument. The following years saw crowds of 600 or more in attendance, with cars, campers and tents circled around the central fire like an old time pioneer wagon train.

Probably no one but Harry Oliver could have initiated such lasting enthusiasm. Once a Hollywood set and costume designer, he moved permanently to the desert in 1946 to escape the sham of city life. And there he stayed, composing tall tales for *The Desert Rat Scrapbook* he issued each fortnight and dreaming up practical jokes to pull on his friends.

Once Oliver delivered an eighteen "karrot" gold nugget from "Lost Pegleg Mine no. 999" to *Desert Magazine*'s office. Henderson described the gold nugget as a plaster of Paris cast of eighteen carrots bunched together, lacquered, and painted gold.

Interest in the Liar's Contest gradually waned in the '60s, until author-publisher Diana and Lowell Lindsay formed a committee to revive it. Their fourteen-year-old daughter Jennifer, who has hardly missed a meeting since the day she was born, deservedly won first prize in 1993, and very probably gave birth to a new Pegleg legend.

Rules are such that anyone can tell a story so long as it lasts no more than five minutes, pertains to gold in the Southwest, and is untrue. Some of the legends we cherish today, like his cache of peglegs, might very well have been products of Harry Oliver's quixotic imagination.

ROCKHOUSE CANYON AND THE LOST EMERALD MINE

Hidden Springs, about fourteen miles north of the Pegleg Monument, gives entree to narrow, steep-walled Rockhouse Canyon.

Marshal South, the "living-off-the-land" experimenter whom we met earlier, claimed to have found a lustrous green emerald in its depth. South related the adventure for *Desert Magazine* shortly before his death in Julian in 1948.

Rumors of an old Indian emerald mine in the Santa Rosa Mountains had been around for a long time, but not taken seriously until Robert Thompson, owner of rich mines in Columbia where most emeralds come from, arrived on the scene with Pablo Martinez, an aged Indian from Mexico. Martinez averred that his great grandfather had worked the Santa Rosa mine. To Thompson, who knew both emeralds and Indian psychology, the story handed down in the Indian's family sounded convincing enough to investigate, even though the rare gem was not believed to occur in North America. Marshal South was engaged to guide the party.

Their climb into the rugged tangle of Rockhouse Canyon proved wearing. Doubling up gullies and floundering along sharp ledges began to confuse them. Pablo grew sullen; reluctant to part with clues. He had told them to look for a ridge with a rock formation that looked like a castle. To South, every boulder silhouetted against the sky began to look like a castle.

At nightfall they made camp in a depression between desolate ridges, but slept uneasily. South sensed unfriendly ghosts haunting the lonely canyon. In the cold light of dawn they ate a cold breakfast and made another cheerless start.

Then suddenly things brightened. Something had set old Pablo off in a wild-goat lope in a direction totally different to that which common sense would have dictated. "Look now for *un cabeza del lobo*," he grunted. "Way up, on top."

But it wasn't "on top" that the "head of a wolf" stood. Instead, it appeared by mere chance when Thompson happened to glance at a fallen rock mass. There, the outline of a wolf's head was unmistakable, even in its upside down position and with a clutter of fallen stones piled around it. Thompson's practiced eye sized up the situation. It was an earthquake. The formation had been toppled from its former perch by an earth shock.

"Goodbye, emeralds," he lamented. He was pointing. The entire slope opposite was a cascade of smashed rock and jumbled boulders. The old mine, if it had lain below the wolf's head as Pablo promised, was now hopelessly buried beneath millions of tons of rock and earth.

Thompson spent the rest of the day uncovering pottery shards and traces of old camps, evidence that in all probability a mine had existed. In one place where sliding rocks had scraped away an earth covering, they found an ancient grave. Amid bits of aged bone, something green sparkled in the sun.

It was an emerald all right, and of fine quality, accompanied by chips of pale green beryl, the substance in which emeralds are found.

Thompson considered recovery of the primitive workings impossible. Even if machinery were available to negotiate the canyon and remove debris, it would be a losing proposition. "For emeralds are chancy," he said. "They occur in 'pockets' that may have been worked out long ago. You never can tell."

So there goes another mine, found, but still lost.

BORREGO BADLANDS AND THE PHANTOM MINER

This forbidding labyrinth of jagged clay hills, the badlands, were formed by centuries of erosion and upward pressure. This is legendary "lost mine" territory, not only of Pegleg's black gold, but others of gold bearing sand.

As the altitude decreases, you are soon looking up at the badlands instead of down on them. In places, the shoreline of an ancient lake is visible. Layers of mud deposited by this lake were later uplifted by earth movements and then carved by cloudbursts into the serrated fans that compose the multi-hued strata of the badlands. Fossil evidence proves that mammoths, rhinoceros, dire wolf, zebra and primitive horses roamed the shores of the ancient lake. Today, late evening shadows throw the scheme into a chro-

Wash Above Oh-My-God Hotsprings (actually a hot water well). Photo by Rita Dahl, October, 1977.

*"**Two Borrego Cowboys.**" Photo courtesy of California Department of Parks and Recreation.*

matic scale of shadowy passages inhabited by coyotes, rabbits, gophers, kit foxes and sometimes an apparition even more alien than those prehistoric ones.

Around the turn of the century these sere, folded crescents were a favored arena for prospectors in search of the area's legendary black gold. But after one dark night, few dared to ever come again. That was the night that Charley Arizona, a wizened and wise old desert hand, was camped on the western edge of the badlands. Something suddenly frightened his burros. Charley walked over to investigate and what he saw scared him too. It was an eight-foot-tall skeleton stumbling around just two hundred yards to the east. Flickering through the skeleton's ribs was a lantern-like light. Charley swore afterwards that he could actually hear bones rattling as the phantom disappeared into the night (or was it his teeth?).

The incident would have been forgotten had not others come forth who also had seen the skeleton, not only in the badlands, but on Superstition Mountain as well, but had doubted their own eyes. This finally prompted a pair of dauntless skeptics to track the skeleton in the badlands. If they had hoped to meet the apparition head on, they were not disappointed. On the third night of their hunt, they spotted an eerie light bobbing against the black sky. As they approached it, the skeleton raced crazily over hills and

Seventeen Palms Oasis. *Visitors today enjoy perusing messages left in the old propector's mailbox just as they have for many years.–LEL*

through arroyos. One of the men aimed a shot at it, to no avail. After about three miles, the winded men gave up.

The glowing phantom has not been seen in recent years. In their quest for an explanation, old-timers decided that it was the spirit of a man who had died on the desert while working his aptly named Phantom Mine. His corpse, reduced to bones by scavengers and heat, had continued to chase intruders around his old claim until Anza-Borrego was established as a protected area and his claim was no longer in jeopardy. Today, of course, we must consider another explanation. As recounted in the previous chapter, writer Victor Stoyanow suspected that the villain was prankster Hank Brandt discouraging poachers from his mine.

Palm Springs-Coachella Valley

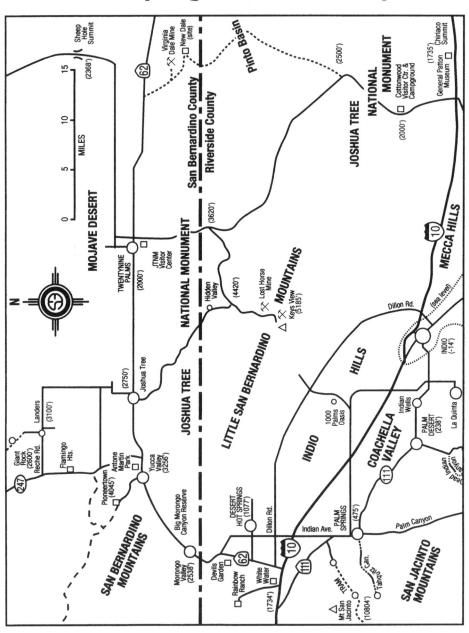

CHAPTER 4
PALM SPRINGS— COACHELLA VALLEY

PALM SPRINGS

Originally called "Palmetto Springs" because of its fine large trees and springs, Palm Springs later assumed the name "Agua Caliente." Later, when discovered by Lt. R.S. Williamson in 1853 while surveying the desert to map a railway route, the oasis became a stopover on the Bradshaw Stage Line until it was abandoned in favor of railway travel. To encourage westward expansion, Congress in 1877 gave odd-numbered sections of the land now comprising Palm Springs and vicinity for ten miles on each side of the tracks to the Southern Pacific and later the even-numbered sections were given to the Cahuillas who had camped in this area for hundreds, perhaps even thousands, of years. The original mineral springs, which now house an elegant spa, are still owned by these Indians and the land is leased.

Celebrated throughout the world for star-studded inhabitants and a glamorous life-style, Coachella Valley has far more to offer than superficial glitz. Read on...

PALM SPRINGS—THE EARLY DAYS

The first white family to settle at Agua Caliente was that of Judge John G. McCallum. He was formerly of Los Angeles and purchased two thousand acres of land and began to promote Palm Springs as a potential citrus-raising community. Then, two years later in 1886, Dr. Wellwood Murray arrived. He recognized the therapeutic value of a spring-fed oasis, protected by mountains from fierce north winds, yet receiving their cool, fresh canyon breezes by night. As Dr. Murray's clinic attracted health-seekers from across the nation and Judge McCallum's agricultural experiments lured new land holders, a steady flow of newcomers began to arrive on the Southern Pacific railroad. They detrained at a former station called Edom, from where they were transported by horse and buggy five miles into Palm Springs.

For a while everyone prospered and then the demon god Tahquitz produced one of his rare celestial disturbances and cut off the water supply. Water had been brought to Palm Springs through wooden aqueducts and stone-lined cemented canals from Whitewater, eighteen miles north of the city, but when floods suddenly changed the channel of the river before it reached the aqueduct, water for irrigating the ranchos fostered by McCallum's land auctions became non-existent.

Groves dried up, people moved away and their houses fell into disrepair. A run-off supply from canyons framing the oasis provided enough water for Dr. Murray's clinic and for Nellie Coffman's Desert Inn tent hotel, which had arisen in 1909, but there was not enough to support an agricultural community.

From then until the 1920s, when a vast underground pool was discovered, Palm Springs remained static. This discovery, of course, precipitated great change. Underground reservoirs built up over the centuries by rain and snow water from the watershed of the Whitewater River and runoff from canyons in the Santa Rosa and San Jacinto Mountains was available to any landholder with the funds to dig a deep enough well. Soon, local water companies were formed and, after Hoover Dam was completed, plans for the All-American Canal were underway. The All-American Canal does not directly serve Palm Springs or Coachella Valley communities lying west of La Quinta, but it freed underground water for their utilization that otherwise would be used for irrigating the date groves and farms of Indio, Thermal and southeastern Coachella Valley that are now served by the canal.

Along with the newly discovered abundance of water came real estate developers, intent upon attracting Hollywood's rich film colony. First to succumb was Charles Farrel who, with Ralph Bellamy, founded the once-exclusive Racquet Club at the north end of the city and initiated a celebrity migration to the Palm Springs area that continues to this day. More and more hotels, private clubs and golf courses followed until land now has become so precious that former wind-blown dunes, once considered to be uninhabitable, are being developed.

Yet the rich bounty of the fresh, natural desert has not all been sacrificed to feed Palm Spring's superficial delights. There is still much on the city's outskirts to attract a confirmed desert buff.

Whitewater River.
*The commercially
operated wind power
generators are a
picturesque addition
to the landscape.–JRL*

WINDMILLS

Entering into this part of the desert from the north, newcomers are startled by the sudden appearance of spindly concrete towers topped by angular wings that resemble prehistoric mosquitoes. Studding the land for so far as the eye can see, these grotesque images reflect man's effort to harness the elements.

They are commercially-owned wind-turbine generators designed to capture coastal air entering the desert through San Gorgonio Pass—windmills in the modern mode. Some environmentalists have objected to their use of the land, but when confronted with the fact that each windmill produces enough kilowatt hours of electricity per year to supply from thirty to thirty-five houses, there is little rebuttal. Ignoring the controversy, one of Coachella Valley's most gifted contemporary artists, Ming C. Lowe, has found their stark patterns a source of inspiration. A provocative interpretation in oil hangs in her mountain top studio located above Palm Desert.

From the windmills, motorists drop down into Coachella Valley, better known to visitors as the "Palm Springs area"; this is much to the dismay of neighboring resort communities who feel ignored.

ONE HORSE SPRING

Hikers seeking both beauty and solitude are not easily accommodated. The more beautiful a spot, the more visitors it attracts. But here is one virtually unknown where stark granite walls house gigantic boulders in a brooding silence broken only by a waterfall's splash. Reached from the end of a dirt road east of the town of Cabazon, a faded Indian trail climbs upward from a natural water tank to end at the waterfall's base amid a cluster of lush water plants. In the springtime, if there has been a good winter of rain and snow in San Jacinto, water tumbles down a 50-foot-high facade to form a stream that must be forded to reach the falls.

The watering place has been known to desert travelers for over a century. Usually it is called One Horse Spring although in his *Guide to Colorado Mines* published in 1862, to aid prospectors en route to the La Paz placers in Arizona, Bancroft referred to it as "Indian Run." Later, when stage companies ran their Concords over Bradshaw's route, they bypassed One Horse Spring and established a station at nearby White Water Ranch.

In September of 1909 the spring saw tragedy when the notorious Paiute, Willie Boy, took the captive girl Elota Boniface there after killing her father. No doubt he hoped to secrete himself until the posse lost his trail. But they found him and, still dragging the girl, he moved on.

Before more modern uses, the canyon was important to Indians of San Gorgonio Pass. The seep at its mouth is surrounded by dead hearths, animal bones, and potsherds. In more verdant days, it supplied food, water, rock for tools and weapons, fiber for matting and baskets, and wood for ceremonial sticks and bows. Today it is a welcome get-a-way for hikers seeking solitude.

WHITEWATER RANCHO/RAINBOW TROUT FARM

Whitewater Rancho, an important overland stage line station on the old Bradshaw Trail in 1862, is a little-known oasis for a pleasant exploratory trip. Located about eighteen miles northwest of Palm Springs, it is rich in history. Here travelers crossing west from the La Paz goldfields on the Colorado River got their first whiff of sea air rushing in from the Pacific through San Gorgonio Pass, thanks to one William D. Bradshaw.

After ferreting out water sources and routes used by Indians to traverse mountains and desert sands between Whitewater and the Colorado River, this far-seeing frontiersman had only to cut a connecting route over which heavy wagons could carry supplies and passengers. His original stagecoach route between Los Angeles and the river included stops at Whitewater, Agua Caliente (Palm Springs), Indian Wells, and Dos Palmas in Coachella Valley.

After days of churning up dust on the trail while crossing the desert to Whitewater, an early stage coach passenger in 1863 wrote, "Down in that desert bowl, exposed to the fierce heat of noonday sun which beat down with uncontrolled fury and beat up with equal intensity from the barren sands, all I could think of was the delicious oasis awaiting us at Whitewater—to drink of its cool, pure spring; to disrobe and bathe all over in its refreshing water. What luxury, what joy lay ahead!"

In spite of the oasis's abundant spring water, shady cottonwood trees and cool breezes, other passengers leaving Whitewater station began to protest over the frequency with which they were required to clamber out of the stage and help lift it from sand as the trail dropped from the rancho down to the desert. Eventually the preferred stage terminus became Yuma, not Ehrenburg, so that stages could travel the Butterfield route through more mountainous territory via Warner Springs before dropping onto the hot desert floor. This route bypassed Whitewater. We shall meet with other portions of the Bradshaw Trail later in the book.

Meanwhile the railroad was building southeast from San Bernardino direct to Yuma via the Smith Survey Route through the Salton Sink. When Southern Pacific iron reached Yuma, a new stage line connected that rail terminus with Ehrenburg directly north along the Colorado River. Consequently the Bradshaw Trail, with its cursed sand traps, was dropped as a scheduled stage line and local wagon routes bypassed Whitewater. We shall meet with other portions of the Bradshaw Trail later in the book.

The present Rainbow Ranch Trout Farm near the old rancho site is a pleasant place to entertain children, or from which to launch a desert expedition to look for buried gold, old rancho relics, or a desperado's cave. You may picnic under its ancient cottonwood trees for a small fee or catch one of the trout leaping up in the pond and grill it on the spot. Temperatures are at least ten degrees cooler than on the desert floor.

Not far from the old white-washed adobe ranch house was a cave where a band of desperadoes lived who did not hesitate to relieve prosperous miners passing this way of their gold dust. Great amounts, in fact, had been stolen by the gang before their hideout was discovered. Then a posse was organized and on one dark night it launched a surprise attack. The desperadoes were shot as they attempted to escape by horseback. None lived to tell where they had cached their stolen hoard of gold. So far as anyone knows it has not yet been found.

This writer was once shown an old journal handed down to heirs of an early trader who, surreptitiously, had done business with the desperadoes at Whitewater. In his journal he suggested that the loot was stashed in a location giving entry to two trails so that in case of trouble, the band could break up and disperse itself in two directions. Not daring to reveal his association with the robbers during his lifetime, the writer of the journal directed his heirs to have a look around "the devil's garden." (See Twentynine Palms chapter.)

An old map shows two roads leading from Whitewater Rancho into the desert at that time, one entering via San Gorgonio Pass (I-10); the other through Morongo Pass (SR-62). It was through the latter pass, connecting link between the Mojave and Colorado Deserts, that the Yuma and Chemehuevi Indians used to come to visit their Cahuilla and Serrano neighbors. The Cahuilla and Serrano, respectively, lived on the desert and in the San Bernardino Mountains. Later, gold prospectors and trappers followed the old Indian trail. The other one, through San Gorgonio Pass and also an ancient Indian trail, was the one used by stages following the Bradshaw Stage route. Gaping caves nearby, tumbled boulders and shadowy little canyons suggest myriad places where early bandits as well as ranchers could have stashed treasure hordes.

PALM SPRINGS AERIAL TRAMWAY

Another major attraction for true desert buffs is the marvelous sky-ride up to the 8,516 foot elevation that overlooks the city. Within fourteen minutes it passes through five distinct life zones, the equivalent of a trip from Sonora, Mexico, to the Arctic Circle. Up at the top, a moving picture describing its construction and the geological history of the San Jacinto range is shown every hour. Other facilities are a restaurant, a snack bar, cocktail lounge, gift shop. Access is offered to a winter sports area, hiking trails and backcountry campgrounds and picnic areas in the Mt. San Jacinto State Park.

Pack a lunch and plan to see more than just the station. A mere hundred yards away along a pine-scented footpath and you are into a primeval forest interspersed with lush meadows, quiet ponds, lagoons and picturesque boulders. It is even possible to explore by muleback. Guided wilderness trail rides are available from Long Valley at the top of the tram, subject to snow conditions, although snow doesn't discourage cross-country skiers in winter.

Chino Canyon, which now holds the lower station of the Palm Springs Aerial Tramway, means in Spanish both "Chinese" and "Curly." Why the canyon received its name is a mystery, but that was the local name for the canyon in 1900 when explorer-writer George Wharton James built a little cabin there beside a hot sulfur spring. During his long love affair with the desert, he was one of the first white men to ascend to the top of San Jacinto.

He wrote enthusiastically of the experience, describing the view from where the top-of-the-tram is today as follows: "so wonderful, so vast, so extensive, so diverse and so magnified—space, distance, sandy wastes, flat plains, water—that it could have been a hashish dream of De Quincy's. It was monstrous, enlarged beyond conception, terrific in its power. Then, too, it was so strange, so foreign. It was a desert, yet at our feet was a great forest leading down to an expansive plain of snow, beyond which nestled a vast lake. Yet, how could it be snow, when heat waves were ascending from it? It was a delusion, a mockery, a phantasm. No, it was not snow! It was salty efflorescence and white or gray sand."

It was in his description of the sand dunes that lay below, though, that he eloquently integrated all of the lore, the mystery, the prehistory and the unbelievable reality of the Colorado Desert into one sumptuous feast of imagery. "From this elevation," he wrote, "the sand dunes assume all kinds of hideous and monstrous shapes, as if the pterodactyls, ichthyosauri, terrific camels, dromedaries, sphinxes, whales, leviathans, wrecked vessels covered with sand, and mossy green stuff that crowds a nightmare with terrors had suddenly become transfixed here forever."

The spectacle might seem less awesome today, with San Jacinto so easy to ascend. But when you are up there two miles above the desert floor overlooking cities, groves, farms, dunes, lakes, mountains and endless stretches of nothingness that reach into the Mexico border forty-five miles away, give pause to the explorers, the prospectors, the dreamers and the doers whose life blood went into challenging this former waste land.

AGUA CALIENTE BAND OF THE CAHUILLA NATION

When the Spanish came to California, the entire Cahuilla Indian nation numbered about five or six thousand. Tribal bands set up their communities in various canyons, but the band known as Agua Caliente, numbering less than a thousand Indians, settled for an area at the base of Mount San Jacinto where warm waters bubbled from the earth.

Golden Checkerboard. *An historic photo of Cahuilla Indians at the door of a hut. Photo coiurtesy of California Department of Parks and Recreation.*

Tribal land in the Palm Springs area is today called the Golden Checkerboard. The transition from a peaceful Indian village to a town began in 1884 when the Southern Pacific Railroad had been given many sections of land (every other section) by the United States Government in payment for construction of a railroad through the area. As the remainder of the land was considered worthless, it was turned over to the Agua Caliente Indians for their reservation.

Years later the tribe discovered that their worthless land had become immensely valuable. After a long fight, the Indians won the right to lease some of their land, but the government limited those leases to ninety-nine years. Then in the 1960s a policy of equal allotments of land to individuals of the tribe was established, which meant that Indian men, women and babes in arms now own a fortune in Palm Springs property which can be leased or sold under government supervision. Many of Palm Spring's finest buildings stand on leased Indian property.

Entrance to the spectacular tribal palm canyons is located four miles south of Palm Springs on South Palm Canyon Drive. The canyons contain the largest natural desert palm oasis in the world, according to Palm Springs Desert Museum Curator Jim Cornet.

Washingtonia filifera seldom grows taller than fifty feet and is thick-trunked, although where water is ample the trunks tend to be more slender. As the tree grows and puts out new fronds at its crown, lower fronds die and hang close to the trunk like a thick skirt. During late spring and early summer, mature trees send out creamy plumes of blossoms which in autumn develop into tiny berries that dangle in clusters from their foliage. Cahuilla Indians harvested the tasty fruit. Periodically they burned the dead fronds to dispose of insects and parasites which inhibited the productivity of the trees. The origin of the wild desert palm is undetermined, but fossil imprints suggest that they existed when the desert as we know it today was partially inundated or threaded with swamps.

Access roads and picnicking facilities are maintained in lower Murray, Andreas and Palm Canyons with a toll gate open between September and May. Once you enter into their primal sanctuary, you are on your own. A paved road winds uphill alongside boulder-studded streambeds and through weird, desert terrain to a mountain-top parking area where you may stop for refreshments and leave your car to explore. A trading post offers souvenirs and refreshments. A sign at the mouth of Palm Canyon perpetuates the myth that some of the trees are 2000 years old. In fact, however, the oldest known tree is only about 150 years.

Hiking trails run for fifteen miles through the deep gorge that carries icy snow water down from the Santa Rosa mountains above to meet a natural hot spring bubbling up through the sand. The palm-shadowed streams and secluded pools nourish over three thousand majestic palms. The Agua Caliente tribe of the Cahuillas had it very good indeed, with hot and cold water running side by side.

The 4,000 palms in Palm Canyon range from seedlings to 150 years old. Many of the giants show traces of fire on their lower trunks. According to legend, the Cahuillas, who picked clusters of their berries for food, burned the trees that belonged to a single family when its head died to enable the departed to carry his berry clusters on his journey.

Andreas Canyon, one of the lower tributaries of the Palm Canyon drainage system, is also accessible from South Palm Canyon Drive. Near one of the most regal of canyon palms is a cave sheltered by a jumble of rocks which still bears smoke charring from ancient Indians. For those who wander afoot, there is more to see—bedrock mortar holes in "Gossip Rock" where ancients ground mesquite beans and seeds; Indian petroglyphs in rock shelters; and stream orchids growing in shallow water beside the stream. The canyon was named for Captain Andreas, a

Old Indian Trail *pointed out by CDPR Ranger Jim Hart near Truckhaven Trail. Photo courtesy of Copley Books.*

famous chieftain of the Cahuillas. Giant grinding stones and unusual rock formations contribute to the interest and beauty of the canyon.

Murray Canyon, another of the tributaries, has a creek lined with palms, but the unimproved trail which follows the floor of the canyon is only for rugged hikers. Graphite upthrusts of strata from yielding sands in this smaller canyon are so spectacularly dramatic they are almost intimidating. In other spots, mortar holes indented in flat boulders near smoke-blackened caves were left by Indian squaws who ground their mesquite beans, wild palm seeds and acorns there to make flour. Named for Dr. Welwood Murray, this is the least visited of the canyons, but one of the best for hikers and bird waters.

Andreas Canyon, one of the lower tributaries of the Palm Canyon drainage system, is also accessible from South Palm Canyon Drive. Near one of the most regal of canyon palms is a cave sheltered by a jumble of rocks which still bears smoke charring from ancient Indians. Giant grinding stones and unusual rock formations contribute to the interest and beauty of the canyon.

Murray Canyon, another of the tributaries, has a creek lined with palms, but the unimproved trail which follows the floor of the canyon is only for rugged hikers. Graphic upthrusts of strata from softer sands in this smaller canyon are so spectacularly dramatic they are almost intimidating. In other spots, mortar holes indented in flat boulders near smoke-blackened caves were left by Indian squaws who ground their mesquite beans, wild palm seeds, and acorns there to make flour.

TAHQUITZ CANYON AND FALLS

Located in the Santa Rosas that rise behind the Palm Springs Desert Museum, this lovely canyon also is on Indian land, but is not included within the reservation so there is no toll fee.

The name Tahquitz was given to the canyon by the Cahuilla Indians because of a mythical monster who once lived there. Mukat, the creator, had empowered Tahquitz to perform supernatural acts believing that he would use them to benefit his people. Tahquitz, however, used his powers mischievously and lecherously and was feared by his people. He lived in a cave up Tahquitz Canyon under a giant rock. There he took the souls of men, women and little children that he captured and feasted upon them. He did his hunting at night and was seen as a giant meteor streaming across the sky. He also caused celestial disturbances. Even today, when his spirit is irritated, he sends "Tahquitz twisters" roaring down the canyon, tearing up trees and dislodging giant boulders.

The prime goal for hikers is Tahquitz Falls which crashes sixty feet down the face of a sheer cliff into a palm-fringed, crystal pool with such pristine beauty that the oasis was featured as Shangri-La in the classic film *Lost Horizon*. To reach the waterfall, an hour's hike each way is necessary. At Ramon Road west of Palm Canyon Drive, a trail goes off to the left. If the road is open, it shortens the hike a bit, but during the heavy tourist season the road is closed to auto travel for conservation purposes.

It has been said by some seasoned desert habitues that in Palm Springs superficiality takes precedence over natural beauty. However, just as a visitor who spends all of his time on the golf course or in a bistro misses the real essence of what the desert is all about, then the desert buff who turns his back upon Palm Springs misses a lot too.

PALM SPRINGS DESERT MUSEUM

This is possibly the only museum in the nation that was paid for by contributions before it opened. The facility contains the Annenberg Theater for performing arts, magnificent sculpture in its courtyards, both permanent and traveling art exhibits, desert dioramas, and an outstanding library of southwestern Americana. When you study a set of early photographs in the Cahuilla Room that depicts tribal life in the old days, you are inclined to conclude that the coming of modern health-seekers and celebrities was not all that bad. Tribal revenue from Indian land leased by the spa has improved the living conditions of its indigenous owners, too.

For desert researchers, the museum houses an excellent library. This writer's own collection of Southwestern Americana was donated to the library some years ago and consists of a number of exceedingly rare out-of-print books.

MOORTEN DESERT BOTANICAL GARDENS

Established in 1938 by "Cactus Slim", a former actor, and his wife Pat Moorten, the Desert Botanical Garden at 1701 South Palm Canyon Drive is the place to go when you want to identify the various wild flowers in bloom on the Colorado Desert. In addition to three thousand varieties of cacti from around the world, all species indigenous to the Colorado Desert are exhibited in natural habitats with rocks, Indian relics, wild birds, desert wildlife and fascinating pieces of desert driftwood collected by the Moortens.

RANCHO MIRAGE

Located at the base of the San Jacinto Mountains, this quiet, primarily residential, community is renowned as the home of the Eisenhower Medical Center and Betty Ford Clinic.

As noted previously, hotels are not pertinent to this book, but the elegant Ritz-Carlton north of Highway-111 at Frank Sinatra Drive should not be missed. Located atop a steep hill, views over the desert are magnificent, but hardly grander than the hotel's classy ambience and antique furnishings. Lunch in the elegant dining room is a special occasion.

PALMS TO PINES HIGHWAY

Where Rancho Mirage and Palm Desert meet, SR-74 intersects Highway-111 to climb from the valley floor into the pine forests of the Santa Rosas. One of the most scenic of its sections, "Seven Level Hill" begins at the end of a long straight stretch that extends from the city limits of Palm Desert. Viewing areas overlooking Coachella Valley are provided from various vantage points along the serpentine climb. Bighorn sheep live in the rugged canyons directly below and are sometimes seen by hikers.

Most spectacular of the view points is the one overlooking Deep Canyon. The sandy wash at the mouth of the canyon has a cross-section of low-desert plants such as palo verde, encelia, smoke tree and chuparosa. And, following a wet winter, verbenas, primroses and a myriad of "belly flowers" (dwarf plants so tiny they require a face-to-earth posture to be seen) grow on the sand flats at the entrance to Deep Canyon. Above, on slopes some 2500 to 4000 feet above sea level, is the favorite haunt of the desert bighorn sheep. The game preserve that borders Deep Canyon holds the largest herd of bighorns in the United States. They sometimes may be seen by hikers.

Dead Indian Canyon at the base of the Pines To Palms Highway near Palm Desert.–JRL

As the highway acquires altitude, low-desert cacti give way to yucca, agave, mesquite and ocotillo which in turn are soon replaced by scrub oak, mountain mahogany and, eventually, ponderosa pine. Many year-round desert dwellers and artists have cottages in the Santa Rosas from which they can commute to town and escape summer heat.

DEAD INDIAN CANYON

A reasonably short hike from the highway just before it makes its first of the seven curves leads to Dead Indian Canyon and its tributaries located on the fringe of Palm Desert. Along the sandy wash, with buckled strata staining its walls and sand- polished boulders jamming its floor, is revealed a cross-section of geologic tumult produced by eons of change. At the canyon's end, a spring seeps through the sand to nourish a stand of *Washingtonia filifera*, the native palm. It is very quiet here. Listen closely and you will hear the ghostly rustles caused by insects among the palm's dried fronds. It was those sounds, heard in the night, that gave this canyon its name. Early Indians thought they were the ghosts of departed souls.

The late Randall Henderson, founder of *Desert Magazine*, early-on assigned himself the task of attempting to map every palm oasis in the Southwest. No mountain was too steep to climb; no rumor of an oasis too remote. Over a period of forty years Henderson wrote numerous articles on the subject and was considered the West's foremost authority on wild palms.

Within a radius of ten miles of Palm Desert and following the perimeter of the cove, he found ten of these hidden oases, one of which is Dead Indian Canyon. Another, even closer to town, lies in Cat Canyon which extends into Haystack Mountain from the end of a road that leads into an area of former five-acre "jackrabbit" homesteads perched on the hillside west of S-74. Climbing from eight hundred feet at the mouth of the canyon up to two thousand feet in the 1960s, Henderson counted four hundred wild palms. These canyons are depicted on the AAA "Riverside County" map.

According to Henderson, these wild palms date back to a period when the desert as we know it today was inundated or threaded with swamps and bayous, with palms growing along the shores of inland seas or waterways. They are found today along the San Andreas fault which extends across the northeast side of Coachella Valley and along the Chocolate Mountains

Coachella Valley Preserve. The Louis Wilhelm cabin built in 1906.–JRL

where little surface water has existed within the memory of man. This suggests that, when the climate changed, the palms survived along fault lines where underground water seeps close to the surface.

Henderson credited coyotes for having perpetrated palms in the lovely oases. They ate the seeds, but digested only the sweet skins. Every canyon Henderson explored contained coyote dung with undigested palm seeds which doubtlessly took root.

THOUSAND PALMS—
COACHELLA VALLEY PRESERVE

East on Monterey Avenue to I-10.

Cross the freeway and take the frontage road north to Ramon Road. Turn east and follow Ramon Road to the Preserve on Thousand Palms Road.

Although modestly designated as 100 Palms on maps dated 1874 and 1891, the name of this charming palm-studded oasis is 1000 Palms today. A large and popular mobile home park development occupies most of the townsite.

Coachella Valley preserve. The Thousand Palms Oasis.–JRL

Established in 1915 as a post office called Edom, after the ancient Asian country, far more than 1000 fan palms are believed to grow in the canyon beyond the town. Some are 700 years old and many stand 20 feet tall, but they are not the only attraction. Tourist also often come to see a conspicuous growth of spanish bayonets (Yucca mohavensis) that grow nearby. The canyon was once the scene for Indian ceremonials.

A dirt road leads to the oasis where Louis Welhelm built his cabin in 1906, having traded two mules and a wagon for the eighty-acre oasis. Still furnished much as the early desert dweller left it, the cabin is surrounded by crystal springs, lush greenery and a stand of ancient, shaggy-bearded palms. It lends itself easily to imagining what life was like for the prospectors and pioneers who tackled the desert before air-conditioning and freeways.

This 13,000-acre last undisturbed watershed in the Coachella Valley came about when the federal government listed the valley's fringe-toed lizard as a threatened species in 1980. By 1984 the California Nature Conservancy had purchased land including Thousand Palms Oasis which, with the State Department of Fish and Game, the U.S. Fish and Wildlife Service and the U.S. Bureau of Land Management (BLM), began the process of developing the preserve.

Besides several rare lizards, the preserve attracts a large population of resident and migratory birds. Hiking and riding trails to other areas of the preserve provide enchanting and relatively obscure respites from the twentieth century. The preserve is open daily from sunrise to sunset and is a real pleasure to visit. It has been said that while living in Rancho Mirage during her brief but stormy marriage to the late Frank Sinatra, Mia Farrow used to escape here to meditate.

PALM DESERT AND DESERT MAGAZINE

The main thrust for Coachella Valley sports enthusiasts today has moved into the Palm Desert-La Quinta area where the big golf and tennis tournaments are held. Palm Desert is a popular resort community well-known to the television public as the home of the Bob Hope Desert Golf Classic as well as the Bob Hope Cultural Center. The city was established around 1946 by the Henderson brothers, who squabbled later in life as to which should be celebrated as the real founder. Upon returning from World War II, the brothers purchased this then uninhabited, naked desert far from the fringe of Palm Springs. Randall Henderson had been publishing *Desert Magazine* in El Centro, but in order to develop the newly purchased property into a viable community, it was necessary to have a post office address. To institute that, the U.S. Postal department required a guaranteed demand for its services. Moving Desert Magazine with its volume of subscribers to the new community fulfilled that requirement. Thus Palm Desert as the home of Desert Magazine became a bona fide city populated by the magazine staff and guest members of the Shadow Mountain Club and motor lodge inaugurated by the other brother, Clifford.

Today the Palm Desert Town Center Mall and the exclusive boutiques and shops along El Paseo are "must" attractions for shoppers, especially in April and early May when many shops reduce stock before the summer slump in tourism.

In spite of the smart shops, fine accommodations and excellent restaurants, Palm Desert attracts a quieter clientele than is found in Palm Springs. Tourist trade in Palm Springs is comprised primarily of short-term visitors, while resorts in the lower end of Coachella Valley cater more to seasonal residents. Much of the social life takes place in private clubs and the "tourist" population consists primarily of second-home owners rather than itinerant travelers.

Hotel information is not pertinent to the theme of this book, but there are two hotels so representative of the resort area's glitzy reputation that they should be visited. One, Marriot's Desert Springs Resort and Spa on Country Club Drive, certainly rates a scenic tour. With lush grounds, cascading waterfalls and gondola rides as much a part of the hotel's interior as exterior, visiting it is an experience you wouldn't want to miss. Ambience here is casual in contrast to the more formal Ritz-Carlton mentioned above in Rancho Mirage.

LIVING DESERT

The entrance to this zoological and botanical preserve lies in Palm Desert less than two miles south of Highway-111 on Portola Road. The lovely natural park extends over twelve hundred acres along the alluvial plain of the Deep Canyon drainage and encompasses six different desert habitats—a wash bed, sand dunes, rock bajadas, barren hillsides, creosote bush flats, and an ephemeral lake. On its premises live over twenty species of mammals, from the tiny deer mouse to the coyote. Fan palms, palo verde, and mesquite thickets provide nesting sites to quail, gnatcatchers, Cooper's hawks, hummingbirds and roadrunners. Three miles of nature trails may be followed with a self-guiding booklet obtainable at the headquarters building, which also houses a small museum. The preserve is open to the public every day from September through mid-June and should not be missed.

INDIAN WELLS

Indian Wells is Coachella Valley's newest city. Incorporated in 1968, it is considered the richest per capita community in the nation due to the wealth of its residents. The only commercial establishments in this business-restricted town are hotels, private country clubs, and a very chic little mall. The rest of the city is made up of private residences. The late President Dwight D. Eisenhower had a winter residence on the grounds of the exclusive Eldorado Country Club.

The name Indian Wells is derived from an old type of well constructed by desert Indians. One in this location served drivers along the Bradshaw Trail which passed this way in the 1860s. Dug by tribal squaws, the walk-down wells extended through an open tunnel far below the surface of the ground and were entered along a series of steps carved out of dirt which led down to the water. Some reached down thirty feet. The Cahuillas are believed to be the only Native American tribe to have constructed wells.

LA QUINTA

Located on Hwy-111 in one of the most beautiful coves of the Santa Rosa's, there are many tales related to the origin of this exclusive resort's name. One is that *la quinta* is derived from the Spanish word for "fifth." When early travelers in wagons or astride crossed the desert along recognizable trails, "fifth day" stopping places were established along the route. It is believed by some that the present resort was so named as a memorial to this legend of desert hospitality. Another historian, however, surmises that it was named for the Spanish word meaning "country estate," while yet another theorizes that the word means "the retreat." Whichever, all are fitting.

La Quinta is reached from Washington Street, which intersects SR-111. Situated in a sandy cove sheltered by mountains that cascade into infinity, the charming La Quinta Hotel arose in the 1920s as an isolated retreat for celebrities wishing to escape curious crowds. Today it has grown into a residential resort community with several private country clubs as well as the recently refurbished charming old hotel.

INDIO, THE DATE CAPITAL

Named Indio in 1876 because of the large number of Indians living in the former railroad construction camp, Indio had more transients than residents until a cross-country highway established it as a business center. Today, its week-long National Date Festival held in February has grown from a modest county fair into a most unusual and popular event, drawing half-a-million visitors each year.

Air conditioning has been largely responsible for the growth of a permanent population in this community, which often knows summertime temperatures of over 120 degrees. To combat heat in the old days, a pioneer named "Pop" Bloomer developed America's first artificially cooled houses. Taking his inspiration from the manner in which desert Indians kept water cool in their clay ollas, or narrow-necked jugs, he constructed some dwellings he called "submarines" that had rounded tin roofs covered with burlap or palm fronds and were then overhung with a sort of trellis. When he wet them down with a hose, like the Indians did their clay jugs, the water evaporated, thus absorbing heat from inside and cooling the dwellings as much as 15 to 20 degrees. The first "submarines" were built in 1921 to house workers for the Southern Pacific Railroad. Today, residents move from air conditioned cars to air conditioned offices to air conditioned houses without experiencing any seasonal discomfort.

For outdoor recreation during hot summer months, they play golf on the night-lighted Indio Municipal 18-hole golf course or take evening dips in Lake Cahuilla nestled against the Santa Rosas at the end of Jefferson Boulevard. This half-mile long lake, with aquatic and camping facilities, was developed in 1970 by the Coachella Valley Water District for use as a terminal reservoir for irrigation water.

THE DATE PALM

Although early Spanish missionaries introduced date palms into California at San Diego in 1769, the fruit failed to mature because of the damp coastal climate. In the early 1800s, pioneers occasionally planted date seeds in valleys of the Colorado Desert to see what would happen. In some cases the experiment proved successful. Because of that, the U.S. Department of Agriculture attempted further experiments with various Old World date varieties and in various locations. It was not until 1904, however, that Walter T. Swingle of the Department determined that the best date was the Deglet Noor and the best place to grow it was Coachella Valley.

The first experimental station was established in Mecca, but because of Mecca's proximity to the north shore of Salton Sea and the threatened flood condition of the rapidly filling basin in 1905, the work was moved to Indio. Now known as the U.S. Date and Citrus Station, Indio has been the center for date research ever since. For many years all activity, both government and private, was strictly to promote date culture. Groves were slow to mature and the members of the Coachella Valley Date Growers had no dates to sell. Today, over ninety percent of the commercial date acreage in the U.S. is in California, and of that, ninety-five percent is in the Coachella Valley.

An interesting aspect of the date is its sex life. Dioecious in habit, separate individuals carry out the palm's male and female functions. Under plantation management, one male palm is sufficient for fifty females. Hand pollination is conducted by cutting the male pollen-bearing blossom stems into short lengths and inserting them in the cluster of female blossoms, similar in appearance, of which there may be up to thirty on each tree. Insects perform the rest of the function.

When stems holding female blossoms curve downward and fruitation proceeds, young date clusters are covered with sheets of paper to prevent blackening of the fruit by occasional rains. A good *Phoenix dactilifera* is more than a product of nature; it is a result of craftsmanship and skill.

Highway-111 that used to pass through plantation after plantation fringed with citrus trees over which rose the slender trunks of date palms, is now lined with condominium developments and hotels. Land has become too precious to support date groves.

Twentynine Palms—The High Desert

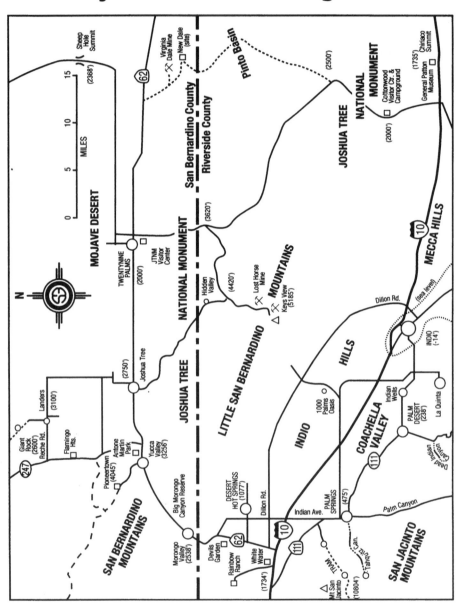

CHAPTER 5

TWENTYNINE PALMS— THE HIGH DESERT

TWENTYNINE PALMS AND THE OASIS OF MARA

This high desert area is favored by many desert-oriented dwellers who find its year-round temperatures preferable to those of the low desert. Attractions include: portions of Joshua Tree National Park, lost mine legends, natural hot springs, the desert's most exotic flora, and a profusion of outlandish individualists.

On the fringes of town, a scattering of widely spaced shacks dot the land, some abandoned, others tidily maintained. These resulted from the Homestead Act passed in 1862 in which tracts of public land were granted to settlers to be developed primarily for farming. The arid desert attracted few homesteaders in the early 1900s. It wasn't until after World War 1, when Dr. James B. Luckie of Pasadena recommended the area as healthful for veterans suffering with lung ailments, that homesteading in the area was encouraged. Soon after that the Great Depression of 1929 produced another rash of home seekers to the desert. Like pioneers before them, they built the required 10 X 12 foot hut of material from the land—clay mixed with water to form sun-dried bricks. A general store was opened by the Frank Bagley family, a gas pump was installed, and the city established.

Following World War II, another rash of "jackrabbit" homesteads sprung up and the idea became so popular that the Bureau of Land Management was receiving over a hundred applications a day for free land. Plots consisted of around 160 acres per homesteader. To hold their land, they were required to make improvements each year. If they failed to, the land went back to the government to be sold, which accounts for the broken dreams symbolized by so many tumbled down shacks. The year 1976, fourteen years after the enactment of the Baby Homestead Act, saw the end of homesteading in the United States.

One fortunate homesteader of the latter era was the late John Hilton, the desert's most sensitive landscape artist. While Hilton

97

improved his acreage, two springs suddenly appeared—one with hot water, the other with cold. He lived for many years in the studio he built on the property with its naturally heated swimming pool. In the 1970s, he and his wife moved to Hawaii, where he died. Hilton's desert paintings today are worth a fortune to collectors. Knowing their worth today, it seems incredible that every year at the New Year's Eve Pegleg Liar's Contest he would throw his "rejects" into the campfire. This was, of course, much to the dismay of all the attendees of those early contests in the 1940's.

Just south of S-62 off Pinto Basin Road lies the Oasis of Mara that played such a major role in the development of this high desert area. A self-guided tour begins at the Oasis Visitor Center. Palms that still remain may be in jeopardy. They need their feet in

Joshua Tree.–CP

the water and their heads in the sun to survive. Over-use of water in the highly populated community has lowered the water table to a point where surface water has all but disappeared.

Even discounting the old Indian legend, one would logically suppose that at some time there must have been twenty-nine palms in this pleasant respite. Its name, Oasis of Mara, was derived from the Maringayams, a branch of the Shoshoean tribe native to the area. The number of palms has varied from nine to thirty, depending upon the local authority. Their only mutual agreement is that there are not twenty-nine. The low desert's native palm is the *Washingtonia filifera*. Other transplanted varieties, or even certain yucca are occasionally confused with the native. When Captain Pedro Fages first saw one in 1772 he recorded the Joshua tree as a "date palm." And therein lies another illogical aspect of this community so noted for individuality.

A botanical, as well as accepted terminological division of "high" desert from "low" is the fact that palms are native to the low desert and Joshua trees are native to the high desert— except in Twentynine Palms and its neighboring communities of Joshua Tree and Yucca Valley. In these, too, it is notable that the human population crosses the borders of logic just as readily as does the flora.

The town of Twentynine Palms thrives on oddities. Its first city hall, established in 1927, consisted of a water tower about twenty feet high supported by wooden walls sloped in pyramid fashion with a single door. Besides conducting business, visitors could stand under the tank and take a shower. Since it was the only community or civic building in the arid area, people came from miles around for water, often awaiting their turn to stand under the spigot.

LEGEND OF MAN-WHO-WALKED-TO-HIS-DEATH

Very long ago Mukat, chief god of the Cahuilla Indians who are native to this part of the desert, promised an old man of the tribe that before he died the god would make him young again. The man, known to the tribe as Old One, had in his youth borne the name Powerful One. Once strongest of the clan, deterioration wrought by age had shattered his confidence—a stiffening back robbed the fleeting speed of his feet, a blurry film deprived his eyes of the vision of a hawk. Squaw's work was all he was fit for now, and that he would *not* do. So he idled away the long days listening to the talk of women while his sons and grandsons and great-grandsons went hunting. And when they returned from forays to show off the spoils and recount exploits of strength and courage, he cringed outside the circle where firelight merged into darkness. Only *he* remembered that his name once had been Powerful One.

As Old One passed his hundredth summer, he became even more feeble. The shaman refused to sing on his behalf. It was plain that the gods wanted him to die. No medicine man could afford to risk his reputation by attempting to save an old man who could not be saved.

And then a miracle happened. As Old One lay dying in his hut made of ocotillo stalks, a mighty figure appeared before him. Even with dimmed vision, he recognized the all-powerful god Mukat, son of the union of red and white lightning.

"Mukat, great god of strength," Old One pleaded, "make me young again. Don't let me die a weak old man. Honor me with a warrior's death."

Looking down from his eight feet of towering brawn, the god replied, "Old One, you are going to die, but before you leave your sons and grandsons and great-grandsons, I shall make you young and strong once more."

And he did. While the children prepared a cave with his cherished possessions to accompany the dying man on his long journey into the night sky, Old One whispered to a grandson, "Leave me now. I want to die alone."

The boy left the hut to tell those who waited outside that Old One's spirit was departing at last. Then, as they all witnessed, a figure appeared in the opening of the hut. It was Old One, but no longer was he a feeble, emaciated old man. Standing erect as a pine, he marched straight ahead to the canyon's edge. Nobody spoke, but all watched in awe as the figure reached the brink. Then, as three sons moved to stop him, Old One saluted the rising sun with upraised arms and leaped into space.

That broke the spell. Old One's grandsons clamored down the face of the cliff. At its bottom, dashed to death on the rocks, lay the crushed, feeble body of an old man.

At least twenty relatives bore witness to the phenomenon. All agreed as to what happened. A council was called to fathom the meaning of the visitation from the god. What the medicine men concluded was that there may be age and there may be youth, but to the gods it is all as one. All time exists at once and all things are equal to infinity.

With that wise counsel, the relatives of Old One left the mountain and went to a nearby oasis they called "Place of Flowers and Trees." And there they burned one of the twenty-nine palm trees in homage to Old One and his powerful god.

JOSHUA TREE NATIONAL PARK— OVERVIEW

There are three entrances to the park, the two northern ones are covered on this route. One is a loop trip from Twentynine Palms which exits to the west at the town of Joshua Tree. The third (south) entrance is covered in the succeeding chapter, Desert Center Area.

Readers who intend to camp or hike in the monument are advised to pick up one of the guidebooks devoted to the park's wonders at the Oasis Visitor Center. In this chapter we are making a loop drive through the northern region of the park where much of the monument's most dramatic terrain is seen before exiting at the Joshua Tree entrance back on S-62. The southern sector of the park is covered in the Desert Center Chapter.

About the size of Rhode Island, the monument was created on order of President Franklin D. Roosevelt in 1936. You could spend months here and still not exhaust opportunities for adventure. Bounded by the Little San Bernardino and Eagle Mountains, it was named for its profusion of Joshua trees, technically *Yucca brevifolia* of the lily family that grow only in high desert regions. They exist in neighboring southern Nevada and in a tiny stretch of Arizona as well as in the high desert of southern California.

When explorer John C. Frement came upon the Joshua tree, he regarded it as "stiff and ungraceful...the most repulsive tree in the vegetable kingdom." Not so the Mormons who gave it its popular name. When Brigham Young's Latter Day Saints were recalled

Joshua Tree National Monument *is best known for its giant granitic boulders and namesake tree.–CP*

from their outpost near San Bernardino and moved across this desert, they interpreted the grotesque appendages of the strange tree as arms raised in command—like a prophet admonishing the brothers to observe the "Words of Wisdom."

Young members of this tree stand as straight as a bottlebrush. It isn't until a flower cluster develops at the terminal bud, or the terminal bud is damaged by insects or elements that the upward growth of the trunk is halted. New growth then takes place in the two or more new limbs that branch forth in random directions from just below the terminal bud. Later, the terminal buds on the new limbs are bypassed in the same way, which accounts for the grotesque diversity of forms the trees take. The tallest known Joshua Tree here is forty-one-and-a-half feet high and almost five hundred years old. The oldest tree, which is the third tallest in the park, may be close to a thousand years old.

Just as there are no two Joshua trees alike, the park's eerie compound of bizarre rock formations is also one of a kind. Spectacular sites visible from the paved road, like monstrous jumbos of sculptured boulders, deserve more than just a photo stop. Take time to explore within their crevices and speculate upon the geologic marvel that produced them.

The granite of which the rocks are formed is called "white tank monzonite" because of the fine granitic formations that form the tanks—"tanks" in desert terminology refer to natural pools of water collected in rock depressions. When hot, the liquid rock was forced up from the earth's interior, but failed to reach the surface. Under the weight of rocks above, the molten liquid slowly cooled, forming granitic rock. Erosion by wind and rain did the rest, wearing away the upper cover of rocks to reveal the granite and then carving it into the grotesque shapes you see today. Nestled in cavities among these rocks are protected coves blackened by ancient Indian fires.

KEYS' VIEW AND VINDICATION
BY ERLE STANLEY GARDNER

If you like panoramas and the sky is clear of mist, a short branch of paved road leading to Keys' View will reward you with a sweeping expanse of low desert extending over Coachella Valley and Salton Sea as far as Signal Mountain across the Mexican border. The road to it was named for Bill Keys, the road's builder and an early miner whose dramatic story is the making of another legend.

Key's View, *elevation 5,185 feet, overlooks Coachella Valley.–CP*

When Bill Keys, a rough, tough, but righteous cowpuncher, came to this high desert area to homestead, his name was known from Death Valley to Tombstone. He had traveled with Death Valley Scotty and been a friend of Buffalo Bill's. He was a straight shooter with a reputation for not tolerating any nonsense.

By working day and night, Keys generated a model ranch from this arid land of monstrous boulders that overlooked Coachella Valley far below. The house he built with his own hands fit so snugly into its setting that it appeared indigenous. Neatly arranged old bottles turning purple in the sun lined a path to its front door. A horse corral, cow barn and chicken-run flanked the main dwelling. It was this man, proudly protective of his young family, his clean waterholes, and well cared for livestock that Erle Stanley Gardner happened upon during a solitary escape to the desert. Key's ranch so enchanted Gardner that he returned as often as he could get away from his law practice to develop plots for the fictional Perry Mason character he had created.

Gardner, who saw beyond Keys' gruff exterior, asked for and received permission to park his original version of a camper on the property. During visits that followed, Keys always offered water and anything else Gardner might need. They became friends.

Then arose the affair of the waterhole.

In this land of spare rain, a waterhole copious enough to meet the needs of a man and his cattle is a possession beyond price. It is the very essence of life. To reach the waterhole, free to anyone in the area, it was necessary for Keys to cross over a narrow strip of a neighboring rancher's property. This rancher, a man named Worth Bagley, was apparently jealous of the vast improvement Key had made to his property and the success of his ranch. So when Keys arrived to collect water one day, he was stopped by a wire fence upon which hung a sign that read: "Keys, this is my last warning."

Keys got out of his car. Bagley was waiting. Just the two of them; no witnesses. When it was over, Keys was on his feet; Bagley lay in the brush.

That was when Keys made a big mistake. Instead of rushing to get help in case Bagley could have been saved, he got his water and stalked off home.

Who can tell the real sequence of events? At the trial, Keys claimed that Bagley had come out of the mesquite with a revolver in his hand, firing. Keys fired back three times with his rifle. Bagley fell. That was all there was to it. Unfortunately for Keys, his tough, no-nonsense reputation worked against him—righteous or not. He was sentenced to nine years in San Quentin Penitentiary for manslaughter.

During the darkest days, Mrs. Frances Keys never gave up. She maintained the ranch and reared her family through every kind of adversity. It was the spot where her husband had brought her as a bride, and it was the spot she would save for his return. So enters Erle Stanley Gardner.

Five-and-a-half years of Keys' sentence had passed when *Argosy Magazine* began to sponsor "The Court of Last Appeals," a

Erle Stanley Gardner *is shown here with J.W. Black trying out the original version of Gardner's "Grasshopper" on the California desert.–CP*

feature in which famous attorneys fought to vindicate innocent persons wrongfully sent to prison. Gardner, an adroit attorney as well as famous author, met with Mrs. Keys. She had little trouble convincing him of his old acquaintance's innocence.

In characteristic "Perry Mason" fashion, Gardner turned up new evidence. Prison doors opened. Keys returned to his ranch filled with ambitious plans to build a dam he had designed during those long years out of circulation. Still, parole did not satisfy him. What Keys really wanted was full pardon to vindicate his reputation.

His seventieth birthday came and went. The sound of a motor halted work on the day he was pouring the last yards of concrete onto the big dam that would capture rains to fill his reservoir. The approaching visitor was Gardner, bearing good news.

On behalf of John Hilton, the famous desert artist, newsman Ed Ainsworth and other prominent Keys sympathizers, Gardner had gone to California Governor Goodwin J. Knight to plea a full pardon for their friend. Heeding Gardner's summary of the exemplary life that had endeared Keys to so many friends, the Governor granted Keys the full pardon that was so important to him for the sake of his family.

Before his death in 1970, I sat around many a campfire with "Uncle Erle," as Gardner's friends call him, and heard him tell many a tale, but I doubt that any other accomplishment of his life gave him more satisfaction than the release of Bill Keys from the stigma of misplaced guilt.

HIDDEN VALLEY

Another point of interest in the park is Hidden Valley. Completely secreted within a wall of massive boulders, an elusive opening gives way to a trail that led to the hideout of legendary cattle rustlers Charlie and Willie Button. Apparently it served them well. The brothers escaped the outlaw's fated noose, only to attend their "last roundup" on a bar room floor after a brawl.

LOST HORSE MINE

A three-and-half mile hike is required to reach the mine, which takes off to the left from Quail Springs Road a short distance beyond the turnoff to Keys' View. The strike was discovered while a partnership of prospectors was searching for a lost horse. Between

Lost Horse Mine.–*JRL*

1893 and 1895 the partners are said to have recovered $3000 in gold a day. In 1895 it was sold to the Ryan family who realized some $350,000 in gold and silver before the turn of the century. By the early 1900s, miners had reached the point where the rich vein hit a fault line and disappeared. It has never been rediscovered. The most visible signs of past mining practices are in the denuded hillside where junipers, pinyons and Joshuas were cut to fuel the boilers of the steam engines that powered the mine's stamp mill.

Hikers in Lost Horse Valley may come upon eight old graves at Lost Horse Well. One is that of Johnny Lang, the prospector who first discovered the mine.

When the monument was established in 1936, a restriction was placed on mining. Previously claimed mines could be operated, but no new claims nor extensions of ore bodies could he worked. In 1950, however, monument boundaries were redrawn to exclude major mining areas, which accounts for the occasional "hobby" mining going on in the area.

JOSHUA TREE (THE TOWN) AND ITS WILY ORANGES

A loop trip may be taken through Joshua Tree National park from Twentynine Palms to the town of Joshua Tree.

Long before modern communication brought the realities of the desert's health-giving qualities to the attention of the world, scheming Joshua Tree real estate promoters devised unique ruses to attack business. With principal clients comprised of guileless rubberneckers from the East, rascals with larceny in their hearts promoted the high desert's empty, unpopulated areas as no less than modern Elysiums. They poured cement sidewalks, laid spur lines and platted townsites into streets with exotic names, sometimes promising a buyer a plot on a street of his own name.

Wily as these entrepreneurs were, the most flagrant of all was a resourceful real estate flake who, after a little judicious trimming and pruning, applied a fat orange to the spike of each spine of a Yucca. "These beautiful trees, so prolifically endowed with oranges, are a natural growth," he spieled to greenhorns, "with fruit that will grow as big as pumpkins!" No Mormon pioneer witnessing the miracle of the Joshua Tree could have been more impressed.

GIANT ROCK AND THE TIME MACHINE

Earlier we remarked that the human population of this region crosses the boundaries of logic as readily as nature ignores the botanical boundaries between deserts "high" and "low." The late George Van Tassel, dean of the West's flying saucer contingent, was a case in point. Van Tassel owned Giant Rock Airport some sixteen miles north of Joshua Tree. The site, although a bit north of this book's range, is so commonly associated with the Twentynine Palms area that we have included it.

Each October Van Tassel sponsored an annual UFO convention (Unidentified Flying Objects), some years attracting as many as 15,000 people. His book, *The Council of Seven Lights* related an incident when a spaceman routed him from bed in the wee hours of morning for a friendly chat. Since then space ships have routinely considered the seven-story-high Giant Rock their "home away from home," wherever in the universe that may be.

Before Van Tassel, who came in 1949, "The Rock" was settled by an American of German descent, Frank Critzer, who left his fishing fleet in Santa Monica to come to the desert for his health. When he spied the astonishing Giant Rock sitting alone on the desert, he opted not to live in its shadow, but to occupy its interior. He opened up a mining claim to hold the land and then tackled the solid stone with chisel and dynamite, hollowing out an underground home in its very heart. With his dwelling completed, he was cool in summer, warm in winter and with tons of granite overhead, leaky roofs posed no threat. So there he lived in solitude, as uncommunicative as his rock. But he was far more resourceful.

Critzer soon found a use for the empty surrounding land. Working alone, he created an airport on the naturally smooth dry lake nearby. Pilots, seeing his windsock, began to land there for one reason or another. Soon Critzer was servicing and repairing planes for a living.

This went on for thirteen years. Then tragedy struck. On July 25, 1942, three deputy sheriffs from Riverside County paid him a visit to investigate allegations that the fifty-nine-year- old man was a German spy. If true, the charges never came to court. Critzer touched off two hundred pounds of dynamite and blew himself to bits.

The rock then stood ignored for five years until Van Tassel, formerly a flight test engineer with Lockheed, leased it and twenty-six hundred surrounding acres from the government to establish an underground home for his wife and three children. The rock already was piped with air ducts, but lacked electricity so Van Tassel installed a light plant. He also opened a cafe and built a "Time Machine."

Upstaging the giant rock as a landmark, the "dome" of his huge time machine, constructed entirely without metal, attracted seekers of perpetual youth. It was not designed as a healing device, but rather to re-energize living matter by recharging cells and consequently retarding the aging process.

If you should visit Giant Rock and are fortunate to find "perpetual youth" at the end of your trek, be sure to inform the writer of this book.

YUCCA VALLEY—ANTONE MARTIN MEMORIAL

Perhaps hundreds of years from now an archaeologist will come upon an entire desert hillside studded with monumental concrete relics that he can't identify as relating to anything of common usage by earlier desert inhabitants.

As a matter of fact, they don't. Antone Martin's legend-in-the-making lies a quick glimpse to the north on foothill slopes overlooking Yucca Valley. It is testimony to a man rewarding himself with his own effort. Martin's fulfilled dream rises in what was his own private park, the Hi-Desert Shrine. It is marked by a highway sign reading "Antone Martin Memorial."

Accepting no help from sects, organizations, churches, or individuals, the artist in the early 1940s began carving his hand-sculptured tableaux depicting the life of Christ. By the time he died in 1961 at an age "over" seventy, he had finished some fifty monuments, financed entirely by his own fortune.

To many observers, the longhaired old man with his white goatee and cement spattered pants appeared as some kind of kook. Actually, he was an accomplished sculptor and anthropologist, excelling in reproductions of prehistoric animals that stand in museums around the world. Where he made his money, though, was in Hollywood during an early career as a top set designer.

An interesting facet of Martin's philosophy was revealed when he offered to turn over part of his homesteaded property with some twenty works of art to the government for a state park. The government was receptive, but in order to cover maintenance costs insisted that a small admittance fee be charged. Motivated by his belief that the Bible is for all mankind regardless of race, creed, color or financial obligation, Martin objected. When the state held firm, secure in having acquired his deed to the property, Martin went forth with a sledgehammer and reduced his former Christ Park to broken cement and bent steel rods.

Afterwards he purchased the adjoining property and started all over again. Today, both parks have been combined and more than fifty remarkable triple-life-sized statues, tableaux, and story scenes give testimony to another desert individualist.

MORONGO VALLEY AND THE BIG MORONGO CANYON PRESERVE

Among the first settlers in the valley was Chuck Warren who in 1873 operated "Warren's Ranch" and ran cattle and sheep to Twentynine Palms. His hospitable ranch provided one of the few stopping places for travelers bound for the Colorado River and mining camps scattered across the desert. As the area attracted newcomers, his son dug "Warren's Well" in Yucca Valley, which became a gathering place for barbecues, square dances and meetings. Even

Big Morongo Canyon.¬*JRL*

so, the area remained primitive. There were only a few telephones prior to 1940 and electricity didn't reach the area until after World War 11.

Located a half-mile southeast of Morongo Valley, the canyon is open daily during daylight hours. This 4,500-acre preserve was established in 1968 as a haven for indigenous flora and fauna. Surface water supports a lush streamside forest which may be viewed from a network of trails. Bird watchers are attracted to the area because of the seldom seen Least Bell's vireo, as well as flycatchers and warblers. Visitors are requested to stay on designated trails and camping is prohibited. Its jungle marshes and tangle of trees provide welcome surcease after a few days of lost mine hunting and tramping over harsh desert land.

DESERT HOT SPRINGS AND
THE OLD INDIAN PUEBLO

This thriving community has long been favored by desert lovers who do not want their atmosphere diluted with too much superficial panache. Things have slicked up a bit in recent years, however. Along with the modest motels and trailer parks with pools and saunas that line its main streets, there are now several country clubs, both semi-private and public, with golf courses. The

Desert Hot Springs.   *The Old Indian Pueblo which is being preserved as an American landmark.–JRL*

community also supports about eight therapeutic spas, most with hotel amenities.

Perhaps the first health-seeker to hit Desert Hot Springs was Cabot Yerxa, who arrived in 1913. He walked in during the night from the old railway stop at Garnet carrying some food in a paper bag and a quart bottle of water, but no blanket. Right from the start he decided that if anything ailed him, it would be cured here, so he acquired a homestead for $10 and then proceeded to keep warm by night with a campfire and by day with sunshine. He was to struggle with nightly chills for a long time before discovering that his property was endowed with two springs, one producing water 128 degrees hot; the other, water ice cold.

After participating in World War I, Yerxa returned to Desert Hot Springs complete with a dream. He would build a castle patterned after the ancient Pueblo cliff dwellings he had seen in New Mexico. The dream grew into a never-ending 19-year reality, continuing until his death in 1965 at age 83, still unfinished. Constructed entirely of second-hand lumber, railway ties and handmade adobe bricks, its four stories sheltered by massive walls embrace 35 rooms designed with different roof levels "to relieve monotony," 65 doors and 140 windows. Under the foundation are several caves. Inside the pueblo is an art gallery embellished with Yerxa's own paintings alongside pioneer relics and souvenirs of the Alaskan Gold Rush which he joined at age 16.

An outstanding event in Yerxa's life were three magic days in 1895 spent as the guest of Mexico's former president Portfirio Diaz in Chapultepec Castle—an event that no doubt inspired his own castle fixation. After that, Yerxa studied art in London and Paris, tramped over England, Ireland and Scotland and at various times secured employment as a sailor, carpenter, cook, reporter, butcher and teamster, covering every state of the U.S. plus Canada, Mexico and Central America.

Since Yerxa's death, his Old Indian Pueblo at 67-616 East Desert View has been maintained by a non-profit corporation devoted to preserving landmarks in America.

DEVIL'S GARDEN

On the northwest side of S-62, opposite Desert Hot Springs is, or was, an enormous cactus patch called the Devil's Garden. Here more species of cacti were observable than anywhere else on the Colorado Desert. In 1905, desert explorer George Wharton James wrote that the cactus "thrived here as if specially guarded." Unfortunately, the spiny devils weren't lethal enough. In the late 1920s when rock gardens were in vogue, truckloads of magnificent barrel cactus ranging from the tiny Mamillaria to the gigantic *E. le covillei* were hauled away. Although the area has never fully recovered, there is still a good display.

PINTO BASIN

Moving to the east from Twentynine Palms, we come to the area's most productive mining district, Pinto Basin. Using Twentynine Palms oasis as a starting point, prospectors staked their claims mostly to the south and east of the water source, often following along old Indian trails. What they sought primarily were veins of milky quartz, stained a reddish brown from iron oxide, commonly associated with gold. When a promising strike appeared, the lucky prospector would stake his claim by marking its four corners with rock cairns. He would then endow the claim with a propitious name, like Lady Luck, and bury an old tobacco can with a description of its boundaries under one of the cairns. Heaven help the old guy who didn't use tobacco!

If his ore sample assayed favorably, he would start digging vertical shafts and horizontal adits that followed the vein, sometimes connecting one mine level to another by a steeply inclined shaft called a winze. Diggings often extended as far as 1,000 feet. This whole area is pocked with them, so if you drive off-highway to explore, take care.

Old Dale Mine ruins are scattered in the Pinto Mountains.–CP

VIRGINIA DALE MINE

A four-wheel-drive trail called the Gold Crown Road climbs and writhes through foothills into the old Virginia Dale Mining district. Actually, three more mines were named "Dale" after the first one was established in 1883. Nobody knows for whom the district was named, but possibly a Virginia Dale was the first child born in the district. As the veins ran out of gold, the miners simply picked up the town and moved it, naming the mines in turn Old Dale, Dale the Second and Dale the third. Old Dale is believed to have spanned the present highway just about where the dirt Gold Crown Road departs it today. Most of Virginia Dale's six claims as well as other mines in the district are accessible by short hikes from the dirt road. If you choose to explore, it is advisable to leave your car on old Gold Crown Road and go afoot because of deep sand on tracks to the mines.

Between harsh desert winds and harsher vandals, remains of the old mines are picked clean. It is interesting, as you poke among the rubble of rusty cans, gravel-filled cyanide tanks and portions of weathered shaft head frames, to imagine the tough lives these determined miners lived. A few were supplied water by wells, often piped from one mine to another, but the early miners transported water in barrels across fourteen miles of roadless desert from the spring at Twentynine Palms. Lumber for arrastres to mill the ores also was hard to come by, which may account for the disappearance of some of the legendary twenty-nine palms at the oasis. Food and supplies were hauled from as far away as Banning.

The rich Supply Mine located on a bench in the Pintos where Gold Crown Road makes a bend to the south was also called Dale the Third. It became the most important mine in the district—so important that it ultimately had electricity as well as the Dale post office, which moved there in 1915. During its heyday, the mine covered 350 acres and yielded over a million dollars in gold. As many as three thousand miners and families are reported to have lived there, but by 1917 the post office closed and by 1919 it had all but petered out. In 1920 only eight residents remained.

A scattering of small mines—the Gold Crown, Golden Egg, Sunset and Duplex among them—pit the region with open shafts. It is advisable to explore this country warily, with an accompanying vehicle and a spare tire.

Possibly the last visit to a Dale mine by a former resident was around 1956 when a mysterious woman in a chauffeur-driven limousine appeared in Twentynine Palms to seek a guide to Dale. When the party arrived as near to the mine as the car could go, the lady excused herself and disappeared with her chauffeur. When they returned to the car, they were toting a heavy strongbox, presumably filled with gold. Back in town she rewarded the guide for his trouble and was never heard from again. Twentynine Palms' population of jackrabbit homesteaders surely heard about it though. Who was she; why had she waited so long to collect her loot; had someone recently died and left her a waybill to a hidden stash? These are all questions to ponder as you trek those lonely desert roads.

THE COXCOMBS—TALE OF THE DROOPY ANGEL

Scraggling eastward, adjacent to the Pintos, lie the rugged crests of Coxcomb Range. Herein lie two desert legends, the first of which is recounted here.

Old prospectors insisted that this mysterious range was rich in minerals, but shied away because of no springs indicated on either early maps or recent ones. Only a mightily determined explorer would dare those sharp peaks that jut from the desert floor like jagged points of an old fowl's comb, and are just as tough. One such arrived in 1902, employed as a wrangler-guide camp-tender with a survey crew making topographic maps for the U.S. Coast and Geodetic Service.

During periods when work slowed down in the rugged terrain, the wrangler would take off on his mule to capture a bit of "fast veal" for the camp cook. It was on one of these treks that he followed a desert bighorn upward into a vertical canyon. When the sheep disappeared around a jagged corner, the hunter worked his way along a narrow ledge to see where the quarry had gone, but at the corner the shelf pinched down to a bare few inches. Knowing it would be folly to follow, he slid his gun to the other hand and inched around to face the wall. It was then that a vein of "dark rose quartz sprinkled with gold" hit him right in the nose. Without any tools, he managed to pry away a small sample with a rock wedge.

To get a bearing for his return, he noted a white blotch, or outcropping, on the opposite wall of the canyon. He later described this as "sort of like a ten-foot-high white angel, tilted at an angle, with one drooping wing." Hence the legend of the Coxcomb's lost "droopy angel" gold.

Around the campfire that night enough of the surveyors saw his quartz sample with its gold to verify the story. Kenneth Marquiss, who told me this story, explained that they had a job to finish so nobody was free to pursue the wrangler's find while the trail was fresh. Marquiss searched in vain during years that followed; by then the trail was lost.

INDIAN'S BLACK GOLD IN THE COXCOMB MOUNTAINS

The second legend was told to me by a descendant of one of the protagonists who requested anonymity so as not to be pestered by gold seekers. It concerns a find of black gold, not to be confused with the legendary Pegleg black gold, that lies hidden in a rimrock valley in this area. The location was cited about sixty miles northeast of Indio, but whether that is as the crow flies or by wagon trail, I do not know. My guess is that it would fall either in the Coxcombs or in the Sheephole Mountains just to their northwest. I have found little to substantiate the story, but then, as the story goes, only two men who ever entered the canyon paved with black gold lived to tell the tale.

One of them, an Indian, had come by a waybill to the golden valley through a story handed down from a tribal ancestor. Deep within the remnants of an extinct volcano lay an immense quantity of gold scattered over the desert floor. The area is so desolate, so arid, that it supports no vegetation. Not even a lizard could survive in its awful heat. The two dauntless characters who lived to tell the tale spent five years stashing caches of water and provisions along a trail in order to survive a pilgrimage into the desolate canyon's depth. On the last lap of their journey, they dismantled their wagon and let it down over the rimrock into the valley with a windlass and ropes. A narrow crevice was found in the canyon's wall through which they led down their mules. Within about five miles of their destination, they left the wagon behind and finished the trip on mules. The dim trail they followed was strewn with skeletons of Indians who had reached the mine, but died on the way out. A small pile of black gold among empty ollas rested beside each mound of bones, indicating that the victims had died of thirst. Our two gold seekers had picked up about $12,000 worth of black gold from the skeletons before even reaching the crater floor where slabs of gold extruded from a ground of volcanic ash studded with nuggets.

The men succeeded in returning to their wagon, more dead than alive, with $65,000 worth of gold, but when they attempted to garner more from the crater, heat and thirst overtook them. They decided to settle for what they had. With his new fortune, the white man purchased an orange grove near Pasadena, California. Not until his life had come to an end and relatives read his private journal was the source of his wealth revealed.

What became of the Indian partner is not known, but a sequel to the story might present a clue. A cowboy once showed up at Mojave, California, with his saddlebags full of black gold nuggets. He reported that he had found them near the Colorado River, but later information revealed that he had found them on the body of a dead Indian who had reached a great deposit of black gold somewhere in the desert northeast of Indio and had died from thirst and intense heat on the way out.

Desert Center Area

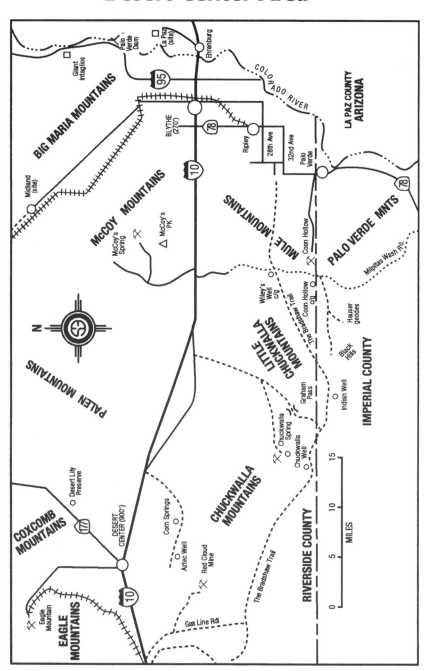

CHAPTER 6
DESERT CENTER AREA

In the middle of what many cross-country motorists call "nowhere," Desert Center provides a gas stop today as well as an historic focal point for intriguing old-time "desert rats" and hermits. Its sands carry echoes of stagecoach wheels and the Bradshaw Trail and marching forces led by General Patton during training for World War II. It contains the southern entrance of Joshua Tree National Park and abounds with hidden oasis.

DESERT STEVE RAGSDALE

After starting life as an itinerant preacher in Arkansas, Steve Ragsdale worked his way west to look for a homestead. Eventually he acquired one in Chuckwalla Valley. There, at a time when motor travel along this route rarely exceeded four cars a day, he opened a service station and lunch counter, offering free water to thirsty sojourners. Thus he founded the town of Desert Center. Then the state paved Highway 60, (now I-10) through his remote desert hamlet and Desert Steve's homestead grew into a thriving concern. One of his sons and a grandson still carry on the business.

If ever a man was infatuated with his own death, it was old Desert Steve. At least thirty years before he died in 1970 at age

Desert Center, "*Dedicated to the service of humanity in mid-desert. Desert Center was founded by Stephen A. (Desert Steve) Ragsdale in 1921. Its main street is 100 miles long.*" *Photo courtesy of Stanley Ragsdale.*

119

eighty-eight, he dug his own grave, attached a bronze plaque with his epitaph onto a boulder beside it, and installed pulleys to lower the casket into a tomb marked by a natural formation of tumbled rocks at the point of Alligator Mountain overlooking Desert Center.

The whole scene stands exactly as he left it—plaque, hole and pulleys, but no casket. When Desert Steve died, a Riverside county official who objected to burials beyond the limits of registered cemeteries, prohibited the Ragsdale family from carrying out the wishes of its departed member. The body was buried "temporarily" in Indio, but these many years later his heirs have given up trying to overcome restrictions permitting old Desert Steve to return to the place where he belongs.

An avid prohibitionist and anti-New Dealer during the Roosevelt era, the epitaph he wrote for himself reflected his philosophy:

DESERT STEVE
Worked like hell to be
An honest American citizen.
Loved his fellow men
and served them.
Hated Booze Guzzling
Hated War
Hated Dirty Deal
Damned Fool Politicians.
Hopes a guy named Ragsdale
Will ever serve humanity
At Desert Center.
He dug his own grave.
Here are his bones.
I put this damn thing up
Before I kicked off.
Nuff said, Steve.

Steve's son, whose reverence for his late father may be somewhat less that the patriarch's was for himself, nevertheless inherited the old man's penchant for individuality. He recently planted, at astronomical expense, a pair of enormous circles outlined by over a hundred towering palms at the freeway onramp to Desert Center—quite a sensation juxtapositioned with the flat, arid surrounding desert. I asked his niece who works in his restaurant if the palms had any significance.

"The idea amused him," was the enigmatic answer. Hopefully there will be enough water to keep the palms amused.

Desert Center. *Picture of the unoccupied self-constructed grave of Desert Steve Ragsdale.*–JRL

EAGLE MOUNTAIN

Cascading behind Desert Center are the Eagle Mountains, named for a rumored colony of eagles. Until recently closed, Kaiser operated an iron mine and mill in a model company town called Eagle Mountain in the foothills. Empty pits are now being considered for storage of Los Angeles waste, opposed by Desert Center's small population.

BRADSHAW STAGE ROUTE

Divided Interstate 10 shortens cross-country driving time, but beyond its traffic zones this country remains much as it was when the freight and stage wagons crossed the old Bradshaw Stage Route in 1869.

Before and following the Civil War, the main bulk of supplies for the United States Army and for Arizona miners arrived on vessels from San Francisco that sailed up the Gulf of California and thence up the Colorado River to Yuma and other river ports. By 1868, however, a cross-country freight route between Arizona's rich mines at La Paz and San Bernardino appeared necessary. Hence the Bradshaw Road was broken from Dos Palmas, near the northeast end of the present Salton Sea, across Chuckwalla Valley to the Colorado River at Bradshaw's Ferry a little north of Blythe. When the gold worked out after a few years, the road was abandoned, but while it lasted the route roughly followed that of I-10 between Desert Center and Blythe. In those days however, stage routes were "natural" ones, subject to change with each passing storm.

A passenger traveling from Ehrenburg, Arizona, to San Bernardino in 1871 wrote about his first stop on the Chuckwalla Desert: "This was supposed to be a station where refreshments and lodgings were furnished. We arrived during a domestic calamity, however. The station manager, blessed with an Indian wife taken according to Indian rites, was deprived of his helpmate, which materially affected the accommodations of the place. Attached to the outer wall was a sign that read: 'Notice—an oldish squaw about thirty; blind in one eye, the left one; a slight halt in one leg; a thoroughbred. She has abandoned the ranch, and anyone who will get her back will receive two sacks of mesquite beans.'"

The stage was detained there for four hours, but up to its time of departure, the traveler complained, no one had come forth to claim the reward.

Skimming along today's freeway between the ribbed McCoy Mountains on the north and the rock-jumbled Chuckwallas on the south you can still sympathize with the haunting loneliness that accompanied the above writer's long, jolting trek.

CORN SPRINGS

About nine miles east of Desert Center a graded road leads south to Corn Springs with an improved campground. Until he died in 1932, a desert hermit named Gus Lederer tended the spring, keeping the waterhole clean while he fed quail and stray burros that came to his cabin. Relics of his crude fence installed around two ancient fig trees planted among the palms by unknown hands are still buried in the sand.

During the annual melon harvest in Imperial Valley, Lederer worked as a fruit tramp at Brawley, earning enough to grubstake himself at Corn Springs for the other forty-six weeks of the year. Although he prospected eternally, he failed to strike it rich, but he always had an open door for desert wanderers and plenty of flapjacks to go around. Proclaiming himself mayor of Corn Springs, he often packed up his mules to make the fifty-mile trek to visit the mayor of Dos Palmas, Frank Coffey.

Corn Spring, once the home of desert hermit, Gus Lederer. –JRL

When Lederer died he fared better than Desert Steve at acquiring a final resting place of his choice. Actually, it was his cantankerous neighbor Desert Steve who arranged Lederer's burial beneath a mound of stones at Aztec Well three miles up the canyon. A second mound on the little mesa there marks the grave of Tommy Jones, a desert prospector who at one time shared a cabin with Lederer.

In 1921 eighty-two palm trees circled the spring and most of them still stand. The gallery of petroglyphs on rocks surrounding the oasis as well as mortar holes indicate that the oasis was more highly populated during prehistoric times. It still affords a lovely respite in the desolate terrain; it is well worth the seven-mile drive to picnic in its shade.

LOST BLACK BUTTE GOLD

A black butte rises in the Chuckwalla range south of Corn Springs that provided a rich find in 1906 for one lone Indian woman. Ill from thirst and fatigue, she stumbled into the old railroad watering station at Glamis, some forty-odd miles to the southwest. A crew of workers on the scene did all they could to comfort her, to no avail. She died, mumbling over and over words they understood as, "Black butte, black butte." In her hand she clutched so tightly a part of a blanket with its four corners knotted to form a sack that they had to pry it from her corpse. Expecting to find a supply of mesquite beans, they were surprised that it contained only a few black rocks.

Two months later the men were discussing the incident when one of them noticed the sack still lying on a shelf. Upon reexamining the black rocks, they discovered that they actually were solid free gold. Black-coated gold usually is associated with the western side of the Colorado desert and the famous lost Pegleg black gold legend, but there have been too many instances of black covered gold reported in other desert areas to discount this legend entirely.

Black Butte was the place most of the rail workers at Glamis suspected as the source for the Indian woman's find. However, in *The Desert is Yours*, Erle Stanley Gardner relates a version of this legend in which the Indian woman recovered and wandered off toward the Chocolate Mountains, inadvertently leaving her sack of gold at the water tank. The Naval Aerial Gunnery Range lies in the Chocolate Mountains today, so the route from Corn Springs would be preferable.

WILEY WELL AND COON HOLLOW

East of Desert Center and south from I-10, a marked road leads to Wiley's Well. Once an important goal for pioneers, it was the first water stop after leaving the Colorado river. In 1862, the stage line wagons along the Bradshaw Trail topped sand dunes and skirted buttes as they traced the first well-defined road across Imperial Valley. Portions of the old road are still visible along the foothills of the Little Chuckwalla Mountains to the north. In this lonely country one can easily imagine the anxiety of stage drivers as they raced toward life-saving water while avoiding bandits and renegade Indians.

Rising like green jewels dropped into a moonscape, feathery desert willows and sprawling palo verde suddenly cluster around a water pump beside a warning sign: **Do not Waste.** This is the Wiley

Wiley Well along the Bradshaw Trail.–JRL

Well campground where early travelers shook off dust from the last lap and geared up strength for the next. Today, RV campers leave messages on its bulletin board to advise friends of their whereabouts while they gather mineral specimens for "show and tell" around the old campfire.

In 1826 a mail service began to operate on an irregular basis between Fort Yuma and San Diego, establishing the route as a military road.

From Wiley Well, a dirt road leads south to the dramatic Black Hills silhouetted like paper cutouts against palomino colored Palo Verde Mountains. This is "rock hound" country, promising untold treasures—primarily opalescent red, yellow and green fire agates, and chalcedony. A special find in the area are rare geodes, often called thunder eggs, whose rough exteriors hide lovely crystalline interiors. The famous Hauser geode beds are in the Black Hills. In spite of the road being graded, one senses the pioneer spirit while passing through the sometimes rugged, sometimes softly tinted pastel terrain.

Coon Hollow, a popular campground shaded by catclaw, a native acacia with spectacular yellow blossoms, lies three miles south of Wiley Well. The large bunches of parasitic desert mistletoe that burden the tree branches may not help the trees, but they provide food for desert birds. The parasite's continued existence is guaranteed by its seeds that pass through the bird's digestive system to be deposited upon new host plants.

Considering the verdant farms and earthy fragrance of alfalfa cultivated in the Palo Verde region to its east today, it is hard to believe that many trappers, traders, explorers, and prospectors lost their lives in search of water in this unmapped territory.

MCCOY SPRING AND INDIAN COUNTRY

East of Desert Center on I-10, an unimproved road leads north to McCoy Spring in the McCoy Mountain. The *bajada* is rocky with rough washes, so is not advised for passenger cars.

In an oasis surrounded with rocks bearing petroglyphs, consistent with other sites near the Colorado River and marked by a giant ironwood tree, McCoy Spring still produces water. Many dim trails radiate from it, some to mines, some to ancient Indian camps and some to low three-sided rock shelters provisioned with rusty G.I. ration cans left over from General Patton's World War II maneuvers in the area.

On old maps it was referred to as Ironwood Mountain. J. Smeaton Chase, in his *California Desert Trails* written in 1920, described a whole forest here of ironwood trees, some twenty feet high with trunks two feet in diameter. Slow burning, most of the ironwoods went toward warming old prospectors' cold desert nights.

W.W. McCoy, for whom both the mountain and its spring were named, was a prominent rancher, packer, and prospector who came to the southwest as a teamster in 1857. In 1862 he brought the first mule train over the San Bernardino-LaPaz road.

RED CLOUD MINE AND THE BRADSHAW TRAIL

Traveling west from Desert Center, a pass between the Orocopia and Chuckwalla ranges is reached along Red Cloud Road off I-10. The road is improved part way, passing through desert stands of catclaw acacia, rusty with bunches of desert mistletoe clinging to it and feathery smoke trees to soften the harsh lava- peaked ridges.

Jumbled upthrusts, apparent from the road, promise rewards for rock hounds, but there is nothing left of the old Canyon Springs Stage Station at road's end except the site. Railroad tracks that periodically join the dirt road once carried ore from Eagle Mountain mines to the north down to a junction with the Southern Pacific Railroad near the Salton Sea. Relics of Red Cloud mine and others still remain at the ends of trails that thread through the area. Frank Coffey, an old desert prospector who once worked at the Red Cloud, later commented, "They didn't need a smelter at the Red Cloud. There wasn't enough gold in that whole mountain to supply a one-armed dentist. All they had was a hole in the ground, a lot o'them fancy stock certificates, and one o' them fast-talkin' city galoots to sell 'em to the suckers."

GENERAL PATTON MEMORIAL MUSEUM

Located in the desolate desert at Chiriaco Summit alongside the freeway west of Desert Center is a World War II memorial with a museum, commemorating the men who trained in General George Patton's Desert Training Center here during World War II. A video presentation provides an insight into the colorful General's career along with special displays of tanks and artillery.

South of the freeway, the Orocopia range begins to rise, as barren as crumpled brown wrapping paper. Its name, meaning "plenty of gold," was not entirely deceptive as many old mine shafts dropping from the ends of dirt trails suggest.

COTTONWOOD SPRINGS, JOSHUA TREE NATIONAL PARK

Further west, Joshua Tree National park's southern entrance is located at Cottonwood Springs. Although two paved roads traverse the heart of the park, over eighty percent of its 1,240.6 square miles is classified as wilderness and must be reached by hiking routes. Similar to the preceding chapter, a number of detailed guides devoted entirely to the park are available at the Cottonwood Visitor Center. We recommend those for visitors wishing to hike, camp or pass beyond the paved road.

Cottonwood Springs, shaded by a grove of palms and cottonwood trees, is a haven for desert birds. In an old Indian camp nearby along Lost Palms Trail may be seen mortar holes worn in stone where Indian women once ground seeds and grain to feed their families. The palms in this oasis are not native, but were planted many years ago. Native palms may be seen at Lost Palm Oasis and Munsen Canyon, both accessible by hiking trails.

General Patton Memorial Museum marks a major World War II army training ground, which is now a memorial.–JRL

Needles to Parker Dam

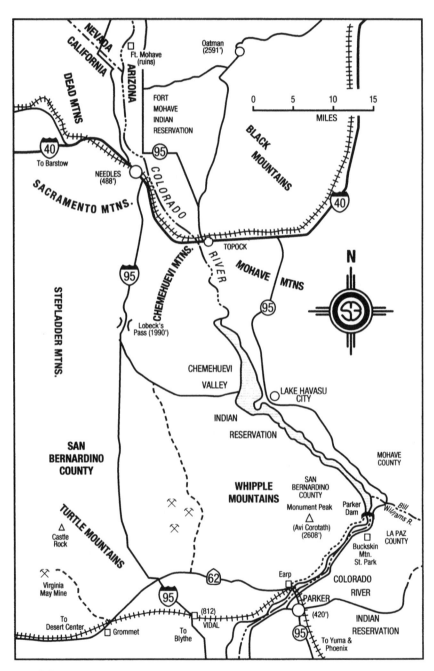

CHAPTER 7

NEEDLES TO PARKER DAM

INDIAN SETTLEMENT ALONG THE COLORADO

Hostile Indians were not the least of the hazards met by early arrivals along the Colorado River. Bands of Yumans, floating down the river on logs with mud plastered over their heads to ward off the sun, might have appeared harmless as mud-balls caught in a current. But when they massacred forty-six Spanish settlers and soldiers at Yuma in 1781, the route was almost abandoned. Cocopahs, Kamia, and other Yuman groups who dwelled near the mouth of the river were somewhat less treacherous, but for many years their thievery of stock and vital supplies harassed early settlers.

In the early days a branch of the Paiutes from the north, the Chemehuevis (Egg-eaters), had strayed into the valley to occupy an area near where Parker Dam is now, while the Mohaves, a more sedentary group, farmed the rich river bottomland near Needles. Fierce warriors all, they combined forces to combat the rush of gold-hungry miners. It required two expeditions, one under Capt. Sitgreaves in 1850 and a second under Lt. Whipple in 1854 to restrain their "protests." Thus Fort Mohave, with a permanently stationed troop, was established on the Colorado River shore north of Needles (not to be confused with a fort of the same name established on the Arizona side some years later).

Today the Mohaves peacefully till the soil and raise citrus on their reservation while the ruins of the fort have all but disappeared. Needles is the focal point for an area described by a nineteenth century California state mineralogist as containing "rock so full of gold and so loose in texture that careless handling shakes out the golden grains." It lies in San Bernardino County and may be properly considered as part of the high Mohave Desert except for a narrow strip of what was once Colorado River floodland which is below 1000 feet elevation and bears greater resemblance to the low Colorado Desert.

An archaeological mystery, spectacular scenery at Parker Dam, a character named Earp and lost mines in the Turtles are part of this area's fascination.

NEEDLES-TOPOCK CROSSING

In 1857, a discouraged Lt. J.C. Ives reported to the U.S. War Department that nature had destined the Colorado River to remain unvisited and unmolested. And no wonder. He had spent many weeks pulling and pushing his iron boat, the *Explorer*, up the river, only to have its bottom ripped out by a sunken rock. But long before Ives agonized over the Colorado's destiny, a Mohave god named Ah-Ve-Koov-o-Tut had driven a great wooden stake into the land and decreed the same thing.

Both were wrong.

Rather than inhibiting future river traffic, Ives' unfortunate adventure had simply proved that steamboats could navigate the Colorado. Soon a whole fleet carried supplies up from the Gulf of California to mineral-glutted mines as far north as Nevada, stopping at Needles to pick up wood collected by Mohave Indians and sold from the river's bank. This precipitated a small trading center that furnished supplies to miners. In spite of Ah-Ve-Koov-o-Tut's promise that all land north of his wooden stake, which by now had turned to stone, would be Mohave land forever, the white man was moving in.

By 1883 the landmark was indelibly established. Engineers of the Santa Fe Railroad elected to place the Needles-Topock bridge there and the California railroad town of Needles was born, ironically named for dramatic pinnacles on the Arizona side of the river. Today, the Mohave reservation at Needles lies a good fifty-mile run from their legendary Monument Peak, located in the Whipples to the south.

The old Needles-Topock Bridge is gone, but the present one that replaced it still provides a "threading through" spot for travelers following Interstate 40 as well as those turning south at the freeway's junction with US-95.

MOHAVE INDIAN CREATION LEGEND

In the beginning, all was fire, and after a long long time, all was water. And then after another long time, the pressure of fire and water made the earth hard and firm. Fire then went up and became the sun. Water went up and became the sky. The sun warmed the earth; the sky gave it rain. And then there appeared two gods, Matavilya and Mastamho who fixed the sun in its place and kept the river in its bed. Thus the earth was ready for people. The gods listened hard. Deep down in the earth they detected

Colorado River, *looking west across "the needles" area of the river, south of the town of Needles, into the Chemehuevi Mountains and Indian Reservation.–CP*

stirrings. It was now time to bring forth those people and let them live on the face of the earth instead of struggling forever underground. So the gods found a soft place on the earth through which they could thrust long willow rods so that the people imprisoned below would know a world above existed. The people understood. They followed the rods and one by one burst forth upon the earth.

When enough people had collected to form a tribe, the gods told them where to go. The Dine (Navajos), they sent to the high-country. The Tinde (Apaches) went far to the east across the desert. The Quechan (Yumans), they sent south to the place where the river flows slowly, and the No (Pimas) were southeast to a place where fruit grew on trees (saguaro cactus). Then those who were to become the Hamakhavas (Mohaves) appeared. Realizing that this tribe was special, the gods determined that it would not have to leave, but could stay right there in the sacred spot within sight of the three mountains (the Needles) and it would be their home forevermore.

The legend has a sequel.

One day there appeared a strangely robed man bearing two crossed sticks he used for ceremonial prayers. He said that his name was Father Garces and that he lived down river with the Quechan (Yumans). He had come to teach the Hamakhavas about a god named Jesus, but although he spoke the Quechan language which they could understand, he mispronounced their names. He called them Hamahab, which in Spanish he spelled Jamajab, since in that language the "j" is pronounced like an "h." After

Garces departed, more men of his kind gradually appeared. Early arrivals called the tribe Hamahab as had Garces, but eventually shortened it to Mahab. Then much later a new kind of man followed, probably an American railroad map-maker, who understood the name "Mahab" to be pronounced and spelled "Mohave." For the tribe itself, the Spanish spelling stuck. Thus in writing, we refer to the tribe as "Mohave," but the Mojave Desert of San Bernardino County is spelled with an "j," acknowledging the Spanish "h" sound of "j."

NEEDLES MAZE

Now that we know that the whole inhabited world started here, Needles' citizens understandably take a passionate interest in paying homage to any old spirits that might still lurk around. Hence today we have a pro-Maze versus anti-Maze archaeological imbroglio.

The Maze is an enormous area of prehistoric windrows raked out of the rocky surface of the desert on the California bank in the pattern of a maze. Scholars have pondered its meaning, if indeed it has one. Those taking the anti-Maze stance claim that it is of modern origin; that Indians were hired in 1889 to sweep the rocks into windrows, parallel rows of rock, to facilitate the hauling of fill while building the old Topock bridge. Everyone agrees that rocks were gathered for that purpose, but irrefutable evidence suggests that such rocks were collected from the *Arizona* side of the river adjacent to the area in which they were put to use, not from the Needles side.

Needles Maze. (Topock) Eye figure, looking north, points directly toward Boundary Cone in distance. Photo by Arda M. Haenszel.–CP

Pro-Maze people, including a number of archaeologists and historical society members, quote witnesses who assert that the Maze was in place on the California side long before the bridge was begun. Further, old-timers describe a huge anthropomorphic figure similar to those seen at other sites along the river that once embellished its center. This figure, along with a large section of the maze, was destroyed during construction of the railroad tracks that led to the bridge.

The Mohaves, apparently having determined that Matavilya and Mastamho weren't the only gods to people the earth, just shrug their shoulders and say the Maze was made by the "old ones who came before." They agree that it must be sacred.

A Desert Watch group has fenced in the area and the San Bernardino County Museum continues to seek information to establish the origin of the Maze once and for all. You may see its remains by following US 40 east from the fringe of town to the Park Moabi turnoff. Then, instead of taking the turnoff, follow the dirt road opposite that passes along the gas line across the railroad tracks. You will have to leave your car and scout around a bit, but once you find it, you'll qualify as a participant in the local archaeological fracas.

Those old Mohave gods may have been first to recognize the importance of the red and gold pinnacles of the "The Needles" as a landmark on Arizona's shore, but they were far from last.

Visible for miles around, they provided a signpost to indicate a safe river crossing for wandering bands of Indians following an ancient Mohave trail up the western shore of the river. Then later, in 1604 and 1775 respectively, the trail it marked felt the uncertain footsteps of Spanish explorers Juan de Onate and Padre Francisco Garces. In 1826, two trailblazers and a horsetrader followed it, namely James Ohio Pattie, Jedediah Smith and Pegleg Smith whose desert trek led to a gold cache.

LAKE HAVASU LANDING— CHEMEHUEVI COUNTRY

About eighteen miles south of Needles a paved road branching off to the east goes to Lake Havasu Landing, an attractive resort run by the Chemehuevi Indians. It is popular with boaters who like to skim across the lake to see London Bridge on the Arizona side or fish in a multitude of "secret" holes where bluegill and bass all but beg to be caught.

The drive from the highway to the waterfront passes through thick groves of cholla, popularly known as Jumping or Teddy Bear

Lake Havasu Landing, the famous London Bridge, located on the Arizona side of the lake.—JRL

Cactus. But this is no teddy bear you'd want to cuddle. Its soft, silvery hairs are really viciously barbed spines that attach themselves to skin so eagerly that they seem to jump. Give chollas wide berth if you do any hiking in this area.

PARKER DAM

At Vidal Junction, where US-95 crosses SR-62, a second access to the river runs eastward to Parker Dam, via Earp.

Until recent years Earp boasted a post office, service station and rickety old shack, once occupied by the contentious pioneer for whom the town was named.

Wyatt Earp, famed for the shootout with the Clanton Gang at the OK Corral in Tombstone, Arizona, came to California in 1864 to drive stages between San Bernardino and Prescott. He was appointed a peace officer along his route during the railway development period. In 1901, he staked a claim at the Happy Day gold mine in the nearby Whipples and moved to Earp to live. The dilapidated shack that once hosted his friends, Bat Masterson and Doc Holliday, burned down a few years ago.

"No great loss," the few locals said. Portrayed in Western films as a heroic peace officer and miner, descendants of old-timers in the area say the man was a cutthroat gambler and murderer. Nevertheless, upon his death in 1929, the Santa Fe railroad and its workers chose to change the town's original name from Brennan to honor the man who already had become a legend.

From this drive along the gorgeous Parker Dam Highway, snuggled between the Whipples and the river, you will see jutting up in the northwest distance like a petrified smoke stack

Parker Dam, named for Earl H. Parker, a Sante Fe Railroad engineer, was constructed between 1934 and 1938 and still helps to control the unruly Colorado River.–JRL

old Ah-Ve-Koov-o-Tut, the Mohave's god's stake that turned to stone, and understand why the Mohaves lamented losing the heart of their land. Threaded among mysterious canyons cutting inland from the sparkling blue waters of the Colorado is a network of Indian trails, rugged enough to challenge the most avid of hikers.

Motorists find the seventeen-mile drive along the river incredibly beautiful. Golden dunes crowd against whipped-up red rock formations. Rustling palms accompany the lap of water. Coyote howls accompany the sizzle of frying fish. If you can resist stopping at one of the numerous resorts with marinas and campgrounds along the waterfront, at least pause for a picnic before heading back on the long desert inland trek toward points south or west.

The Parker Dam Highway ends at the dam site, named for Earl H. Parker, a Santa Fe Railroad engineer who ran the line for the Parker Cut-off in 1905-06. Constructed between 1934 and 1938, it is one part of a water system of storage and diversion structures built by the U.S. Bureau of Reclamation to control and regulate the once unruly Colorado River. An interesting self-guided tour of the dam is available in its visitor center.

After touring the dam, you may either return to Vidal Junction on the California side the way you came, or cross to Arizona at the dam site and follow along the opposite side of the river as far as the town of Parker, where a bridge re-crosses the river and returns to California.

Parker Dam Highway, a view of one of the many campgrounds, this one is looking west towards the Whipple Mountains on the California side (1972).–LEL

TURTLE MOUNTAINS AND THE LOST ARCH MINE

This section of the Mojave may seem long and dreary for those not in tune with empty desert terrain. Those who are trained to see the desert with a knowledgeable eye find a deep thrill in the transition from Rice Valley's frozen dunes to the south, like static waves in a static sea, to the slopes of the Turtle Mountains to the north, and the powerful folds that radiate from granite mountains to the west. During early spring, wildflowers spill over the sand and cactus blossoms soften the severe scapes.

Beguiling is the word for the classic Lost Arch Mine legend of the Turtles. Beguiling, because nobody is certain whether the "arch" that identified the rich placer mine was a natural rock formation, a man-made adobe, or both. Somewhere near the east end of the range hides a lost placer originally worked by a small party of Mexicans. En route to the rich placers of La Paz on the Colorado River, they made camp beside a wash in the Turtles following a rainstorm. When the sun arose the following morn, the sandy bottom of the wash glittered with gold. No longer interested in La Paz, the Mexicans hastened to set up their own operation on a mesa above the wash. For shelter, they constructed two separate adobe rooms joined by an extended roof in the shape of an arch. Everything went nicely until summer. Then the searing desert sun dried up a nearby spring, thus curtailing the sluicing operation necessary to the recovery of placer gold. Undaunted, the Mexicans secreted their equipment and moved to other fields, intending to return in the fall.

In true "lost mine" tradition, they failed to get back together again and various members who tried to locate it alone were unsuccessful. Eventually even the adobe walls of their huts melted in the rains, leaving only the arch to mark the site. The last person to report its condition was a German naturalist named Kohler who camped there in 1900, unaware of the significance of the former structure.

That was the first of three legendary Lost Arch Mines in the Turtles.

In the 1900s, some years after the Mexicans departed, an old miner was found murdered in the general area. In his hand was grasped a sketch of an eroded arch formation with a vague waybill that his friends claimed he had written while dying in order to direct them to a rich strike he was in the process of developing. Was his sketch meant to suggest the arch constructed by the early miners, or was it depicting a natural formation that marked a separate strike?

Many have looked; none have found. In 1963 the late Erle Stanley Gardner, creator of Perry Mason detective books and television shows, employed a helicopter to look for it. I accompanied Gardner in search of a number of other lost mines by helicopter, but was unable to join this attempt. He told me later that they found several natural arches in the east end of the Turtles, but in places too rugged to land the helicopter. Hunting lost mines was

Turtle Mountains. *The foothills "where the lost Arch Mines still are not found."–CP*

Gardner's escape from the relentless pressure of deadlines. We always meant to investigate the Turtles further, then time ran out.

But that isn't the end of the lost arches. Still remaining are relics of a mine operated by Charlie Brown, a well-known prospector who worked the Turtles in the 1930s. He named his mine "The Lost Arch" just to fool other prospectors into thinking the lost had been found—and claimed. I've been told that remnants of his cabin still stand, but considering that operation "Desert Strike" by the U.S. Army during World War II obliterated old trails while crisscrossing the Turtles with tanks, it is unlikely that any clues to the location of his placer will be found.

In addition to lost mines, the volcanic Turtles also yield booty for rockhounds. Agates, jasper, creamy chalcedony roses, feldspar and massive quartz predominate, with some fire agate among the chalcedony fields. The finest field of chalcedony roses lies around Mopah Peak on the eastern end of the range.

CP

Blythe to Yuma

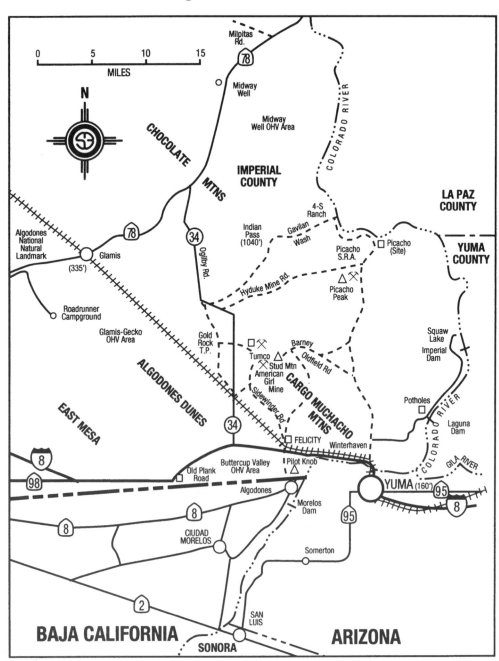

CHAPTER 8

BLYTHE TO YUMA

FROM THE SPANISH MAIN
TO THE RIO COLORADO

Mysterious intaglios, historic trails, photogenic sand dunes, a noted trading post, lost gold, mine ruins, a new town and forgotten Spanish missions render this area among my favorite of desert treks.

Vacillating like the tail of a runaway kite, the Colorado River that gives this sector of the Sonoran Desert its name, has cut swaths in every direction from its present course. It was those swaths that effected the often controversial, occasionally whimsical, destiny of the daring pioneers, prospectors and explorers who left their monumental legacies preserved in its desert sands.

Francisco de Ulloa set the scene when three Spanish vessels under his command sailed up the coast from Acapulco in 1539 and discovered that there was a gulf, now known as the Gulf of California. Discovery of the Colorado River which emptied into that gulf, however, had to wait until May of 1540 when Pedro de Alarcon, hoping to assist Coronado's expedition in search of the Seven Golden Cities of Cibola, proceeded northward beyond the point where Ulloa had turned back. The exact distance up river that Alarcon traveled has never been determined, but it is doubtful that he glimpsed the Colorado Desert. So it was Melchior Diaz, following Alarcon by land to effect an aborted rendezvous, who is credited with being the first white man to set foot upon the Colorado Desert.

Diaz reported that the earth trembled, the sand was "hot as ashes and the whole country was desolate and forbidding." After four days he fled its scorching weariness. On the return trek to Mexico, he succumbed to a wound caused by a freak accident when he fell from his horse and was impaled on a spear.

Following these hesitant 16th Century approaches, the Colorado River and its desert remained the uncontested domain of its native Indians for well over a century.

BLYTHE

The town of Blythe acquired its name from Thomas Blythe, an unfortunate Englishman who filed claims on 40,000 acres along the Colorado River in 1877 under the Swamp and Overflow Act, believing the area would turn into a new Nile Valley. Instead, it almost turned into a catastrophe.

Before he could develop his land, Blythe died of a paralytic stroke. Then litigation tied up the property for twenty-one years before the estate was sold to the syndicate that platted the town.

Farmers, drawn here by the promise of rich overflow land, found they had to contend with annual sprees by the Colorado River cutting through the levees. Until recent years there were still old-timers who remembered when a gopher hole was enough to start a trickle of water through the dike that would surge into a ten-foot breach of rushing water before even being discovered. Then, all through the night, every able-bodied man among them worked at filling burlap bags with dirt to pile against the crumbling bank in an effort to prevent total disaster. Hoover Dam, of course, put an end to the struggle. In the meantime residents had spent almost five million dollars fighting the river, losing ninety per cent of their property to the state because of the inability to liquidate the immense debt the river had forced upon them.

Today, Blythe is a busy agricultural center, surrounded for miles around with green alfalfa fields. Located on Interstate 10, it also provides a routine stop for motorists, with modern motels and restaurants evident along its main thoroughfare.

GIANT INTAGLIOS

Eighteen miles north of Blythe is a monument on S-95 indicating the location of a set of prehistoric giant intaglios scraped into the rock on a mesa above the present highway. The actual site, contained within a fence, lies a short distance from the highway along a dirt road to the west, while another site is about a half-mile northwest of the first one. These effigies, along with others less accessible on the Arizona side of the river, present a mystery still unsolved by archaeologists.

They were discovered in the fall of 1930 by George Palmer, a Nevada airport operator. Palmer had crossed the Riverside Mountain heading south to Blythe when he saw marks on the ground which resembled horse tracks. Since he was flying at an altitude of 5,000 feet, he calculated that each hoof mark below would have to be at least three feet in diameter to be visible from his plane. While

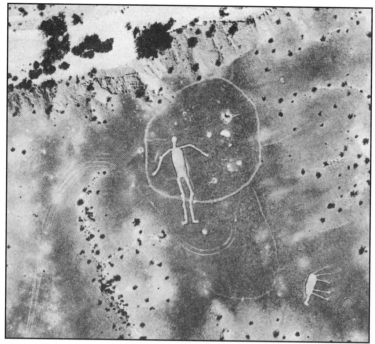

Giant Geoglyphs. *An aerial view of a giant figure near Blythe. Circa 1950s. Photo by Bert Watts.–CP*

speculating upon the monstrous animal this would represent, he was even more astonished to look down again and see the outline of a man stretched out on his back on top of a mesa. Palmer circled the figure and dropped to 2,000 feet. He then could discern the figures of a horse and a coiled snake adjacent to the man, all of gigantic size.

Palmer landed at Blythe and immediately set out to question old prospectors in the area about the strange figures. Many had tramped through the Big Marias where the mesa bearing the human and animal figures was located, but none had ever seen or heard of either the tracks or the figures, which is no wonder. Their immense sizes are so exaggerated that they would have been apparent only to God and birds before man took to the air.

Although Palmer photographed and reported them to the curator of history at the Los Angeles County Museum, a bona fide expedition was not launched until 1952 when General of the Army George C. Marshall rediscovered them while on a desert air maneuver. At this time the National Geographic and the Smithsonian

Institute sent archaeologists who subsequently located additional sites on the opposite side of the river in Arizona. They did not, however, discover Palmer's gigantic horse tracks.

The largest of the Blythe intaglios is of a woman 171 feet long with outflung arms spanning a distance of 158 feet. Her male companion measures ninety-five feet. The animal figure is believed to be a horse, long legged and shaggy tailed. If it is a horse, the effigies would appear to post-date 1540, as that is when the Spanish conquistadors introduced horses to the Southwest. Our native Pleistocene horse became extinct 10,000 years ago.

Subsequent findings, however, do not entirely discount the possibility that they are older than formerly believed. Larry Loendorf of the University of North Dakota and Ron Dorn of Arizona State University recently used advanced radiocarbon techniques to date organic matter that grew on gravel in the Blythe figures and found that the artworks were created about A.D. 890. Further, rather than a horse as believed in the past, Jay von Werlhof of California's Imperial Valley College thinks that they represent Kumastamho, the creator, and his mountain lion helper—figures still meaningful to the Mohave and Quechan tribal culture.

ALGODONES DUNES

Hugh Osborn County Park was established to preserve these magnificent dunes in an undisturbed state and to protect rare plant and

Algodones Dunes.   *View of the sand hills 27 miles west of Yuma. Photo courtesy of United States Department of Agriculture.*–CP

animal species that survive in them. The area is closed to vehicle travel, but to the south of the highway from Glamis an open recreational area provides spills and thrills for thousands of dune buggy drivers.

Like a thrashing sea of beige waves, some of the dunes rise three hundred feet from the desert floor. Early travelers called them "walking hills" because they constantly changed size and shape. Within each sandy hill lies a heart. It may be a root, a rock, a broken wagon wheel, but always a barrier was there to collect wind-blown particles of sand that grew larger and larger until they melded one into the other to form this sea of sand. Then, with winds beating at them continually from the west, lifting sand up the sloping sides and dropping it over the top, westward slopes were eaten away while eastern ones advanced, traveling about a foot per year.

The age of these dunes is unknown, but they are made up of sands derived from the disintegration of surrounding mountains as well as the breakdown of sandstones of old Tertiary marine beds left from a time when the water level of an ancient sea filled the Salton basin much higher than the Salton Sea does today.

As arid as they appear, they do sustain instances of life, like the rare silver-leafed dune sunflower and the silvery zebra-tailed lizard (*Callisaurus draconoides*) that occasionally is seen weaving fancy curves through the sand during its mating season.

And yes, they also sustain a lost treasure!

ALGODONES GOLD LEGEND

In 1917 a violent sandstorm suddenly arose to assault a lone prospector trudging over the dunes alongside his burro. "Assault" is the only word to describe the chaos it caused. The poor burro simply disappeared in a barrage of sand, as did the prospector's water and supplies. Fortunately he was near the fringe of the dunes where he could lie face down while sand blew over without burying him completely. At last the sandstorm subsided and its exhausted victim staggered off in the direction of the railroad stop at Ogilby, hoping to get there before dying of dehydration.

En route, somewhere between the dunes and his destination, he walked over an area of hardpan. Seasoned prospector that he was, not even a threat of death stopped him from pausing to gather seventeen-and-a-half pounds of wind-scoured stones which he recognized as gold.

Finally arrived at the station, foggy in the head and more dead than alive, he showed the agent his find and attempted to sketch a rough map of the gold's location. In view of his condition, all the stationmaster could do was put him on a train destined for Los Angeles where the prospector could get medical attention. As a result of extreme dehydration, the man never recovered to retrace his steps. Today, the Algodones gold probably lies in the buried footprints of those "walking" dunes.

INDIAN PASS ROAD

Continuing south from the junction, it is possible to enter into the Picacho State Park from Ogilby Road as well as from another entrance further south off I-8 near Winterhaven. You may wish to enter one way and exit the other. The circuit trek is about sixty miles, all on a sometimes improved, but winding four wheel drive dirt road.

Before heading into Indian Pass Road, even backcountry vehicles are advised to continue on Ogilby Road for five miles to the Gold Rock Trading Post to inquire of road conditions. Summer storms have been known to wreck havoc with sections of Indian Pass. However, if storms have not disturbed the improved road from S-34, a loop trip through Picacho from the Indian Pass Road entrance to the southern Winterhaven exit is one of the most exciting scenic trips on the Colorado Desert. We do not recommend making this loop through Indian Pass in a passenger car, but it has been done under good road conditions.

Those with back-country equipment who choose to enter the Picacho State Recreation Area along this route, instead of entering from Winterhaven will then exit at Winterhaven, and meet I-8.

Evidence of more than one culture along Indian Pass Road clearly establishes it as a main route of ancient travel, possibly beginning with early San Dieguito man who existed over 9,000 years B.C., according to Malcolm Rogers, former staff archaeologist at the San Diego Museum of Man. Hikers following old trails through the rocky desert-varnished terrain may come upon an alignment of boulders over a hundred feet long that crosses one trail after having followed alongside another. This possibly operated as a barrier to prevent spirits of an earlier departed culture from crossing over to a later tribe's own trails. Prehistoric Yumans, who arrived on the scene about 1,000 A.D., usually cut their trails parallel to ancient ones, rather than travel in the footsteps of the dead. Exceptions, of course, were through narrow mountain passes where all trails converged into one.

Indian Pass Road. Rock circles, sometimes called "sleeping circles" are apparent alongside the road.–CP

A number of circles formed by lumps of rocks outlining cleared centers are apparent alongside the road. These are sometimes called "sleeping circles" within which naked, early Indians may have curled up and huddled together for warmth at night. The Yumans, who came later, were more modest. Their traditional rock-rimmed dwellings left an opening for a doorway and were roofed with reed thatching. In addition to "sleeping circles," there are other smaller ones that I have seen in desert areas as far from the Colorado River as Anza-Borrego. My own deduction is that they represented primitive "safety deposit vaults" in which a cache of stones or tokens for trade was protected by an ancient honor system until its owner returned to the area. Another explanation is that the chips of quartz, blue desert lapis and agate deposited into the circles were cast there by superstitious ancients making an offering, like modern man might toss a coin into a fountain for good luck. Another theory suggests that the "sleeping circles" may have been used as hunting blinds.

When Indian Pass Road reaches Gavilan Wash, a dangerous downhill trek that leads to the Colorado River, prudent drivers may prefer to return to Ogilby Road and approach those spectacular Picachos that dominate the landscape like globs of custard from the tamer Winterhaven entrance.

GOLD ROCK TRADING POST AND TUMCO GHOST TOWN

Originally built by the late Carl Walker and his wife who in the late '30s owned the Tumco Mine and ghost town east of the ranch, Gold Rock is now maintained as a trading post and rock hound meeting

Gold Rock Trading Post, originally built in the late '30s, is now maintained as a trading post.—CP

ground. The trading post is a veritable museum of desert memorabilia with Indian stone tools, rocks with petroglyphs, old mining equipment, crystal spheres, desert driftwood and every kind of rock indigenous to the desert. I prize an enormous amethyst geode I purchased here.

The late Bob Walker came to the area to homestead with his parents in 1920. They had expected to mine, but when they finally found water it proved more lucrative to supply the miners with water than to do the work themselves. At that time miners were extracting gold from tailings left from more productive days. At age thirty-three Walker met his future wife Scotty while on a visit to the mid-west. He enticed her to the desert, they married, and in spite of heat and wind-blown sand, she never had a regret and lived until her death in the neat, attractive house with its wide veranda and rock walls.

There is no known documentary evidence, but there are indications that gold was discovered in the Cargo Muchachos three quarters of a century before Marshall found nuggets in the Mother Lode country and started the '49ers gold rush to California. J. Ross Browne and William Blake, both early explorers and historians, wrote that gold was known along the Colorado River in the 1770s, and Paul Henshaw, writing in the *California Journal of Mines and Geology* in 1942 stated that mining was first carried on in the Cargo Muchachos in 1780 with the founding of Spanish settlements on the Colorado River.

Further, Yuma (or Quechan) Indian historians recount tales of tribal ancestors forced to dig gold for the early Spaniard explorers who named the Cargo Muchacho Mountains to commemorate an occasion when one of their children, imitating his gold-seeking father, returned to camp carrying ore which proved rich in gold. (Muchacho means boy in Spanish.)

The mine, Tumco, was named for the initials of The United Mines Company. It sprawled east of the paved road along a dirt trail that bears a marker, but its buildings have crumbled into the earth and there is nothing to see there now. Discovered by a Swedish trackwalker and first known as Hedges, its ghost indicates a far greater population than exists in this part of the desert today. During its time of glory, Tumco boasted of 3,000 residents who frequented four saloons along Stingaree Gulch. Mines in the district were worked from 1892 to 1909 steadily, and then later from 1913 to 1916. The most famous among them were the Golden Queen, the Golden Cross and the Golden Crown, each operating twenty-four hours a day. In 1896 Hedges peaked, boasting of a store, hospital, several bordellos, a casino and seven saloons.

Of the saloons, perhaps the most popular was the Stingeree run by Billy Horan, who also performed as the town's undertaker and constable. Once impaled against his saloon wall with a knife thrust through each arm and faced by a surly Mexican, Horan escaped death only through the grace of a friend whose pistol shot had killed the rampaging attacker.

The demise of mines in the Tumco district was due to over-expansion without first developing reserves. The forty-stamp mill had been processing 120 tons of ore each twenty-four hours until 1910, when the facility was augmented with a 100-stamp mill at enormous cost.

Without enough reserves to feed the new giant mill, Tumco went broke. Equipment was sold for junk, metal was salvaged from mills, rails wrested from their bedding and hoses carted away for scrap. For awhile the site was a ghost town, and then vandals even put an end to that.

LOST GOLD IN THE CARGO MUCHACHOS: SULLIVAN AND MULE SHOE

Jim Sullivan, a big Irishman who managed Billy Horan's Stingaree saloon at Hedges in the mid '90s, hired an Indian swamper (clean-up man) one hot summer. After watching him awhile, Sullivan grew suspicious of the implausible amount of gold ore the swamper seemed to have at his disposal. Whether by threat or wile, Sullivan finally cajoled the swamper into agreeing to lead him to the source of his ore.

In spite of summer heat, the two men loaded a mule with supplies and set forth, stopping only long enough to get the mule shoed at a small blacksmith shop along the Yuma freight road east of the Cargos. It, too, was maintained by Sullivan's boss, the enterprising Billy Horan.

Once arrived at the richly veined ledge, they set to work with pick and shovel. Soaked with sweat and finding his canteen empty, Sullivan took a deep gulp from one of the two old kerosene cans that held their water supply. Suddenly he gagged, spewing water onto the ground. The Indian, whose duty had been to fill the kerosene cans with water had neglected to rinse them out first. In a flash of madness, Sullivan aimed his revolver and shot both cans full of holes. The swamper was lucky that it wasn't aimed at him.

As the last of their water vanished into hot sand, there was nothing to do but backtrack to the nearest supply, Billy Horan's blacksmith shop. Barely alive, but still clutching a sample of his gold, Sullivan arrived astride the mule. The swamper had vanished as wholly as their water had been swallowed by sand. Horan loaded the dehydrated Irishman into a buckboard and hauled him back to Hedges.

When assayed, the values of Sullivan's ore samples were $1000 a ton and higher in gold. The ore appeared to be of two kinds: yellowish-red with limonite, and chocolate brown with hematite. Iron and gold in quartz is paradoxically unlike ore in other strikes either in Hedges or elsewhere in the Cargos or Picacho. Sullivan was shipped by train to a California hospital to recover from his ordeal, but he hadn't given up yet.

The late desert historian Harold Weight once interviewed Billy Horan for *Desert Magazine*. Horan recalled that after Sullivan recovered, he returned to the Cargos a number of times until his last search in 1920. On one occasion Horan accompanied him. Uncertain of the ledge's location without the Indian guide, Sullivan had tried to retrace their original route from Horan's blacksmith shop where they had begun. Estimating that they had traveled about fifteen miles from the shop, this effort led them across the Picacho road near Pebble Mountain. They searched in vain, until supplies ran out.

According to Horan, it is unlikely that the site would be closer to the river than Pebble Mountain or Sullivan and the Indian would have gone there for water instead of backtracking. A dearth of water in the area has also caused others to turn back. Until his dying day Horan remained convinced that Sullivan's golden ledge still awaited a finder. The unique composition of the ore would have given away the secret had it been found.

Could Sullivan's lost gold have come from the same gold-veined ledge that gave birth to the legend of the Lost Mule Shoe Gold?

Around the same time that Sullivan was recovering from his harrowing experience, an extremely ill man whose name history has forgotten was setting out on horseback from Picacho to get treatment at the Sawtell Veterans' Hospital near San Bernardino. As his route passed through the rugged Cargo Muchachos, he grew so weak that he fell to the ground. When consciousness returned, he found himself lying on a bed of nuggets at the base of a ledge veined with gold. Too weak to do anything about it then, he marked the place as best as he could by leaving his vest on the ledge held in place by a mule shoe. He then continued along his westward route. By the time he reached the oasis at Dos Palmas, the ailing man knew that his health would never permit a return trek. There, he told of his valuable find to some other wayfarers who saw him safely to the veterans' hospital, where he soon died.

The gold he found himself lying on might well have been that removed from the ledge earlier by Sullivan, before the Irishman's frantic exodus after drinking kerosene-tainted water. Whatever, neither ledge has been found.

AMERICAN GIRL MINE

The now defunct American Girl Mine, reached by a dirt road some four miles east of Gold Rock Trading Post, was developed later than Tumco and also drew a lot of attention to the Cargo Muchachos. Today, melted adobe walls and broken foundations are about all that remain of the old Tumco works. In recent years mica and pyrophylite, used as bases in paints, insecticides and plastics, have been mined in the area.

The area is currently fenced off and guarded. Contact the Bureau of Land Management (BLM) in El Centro for further information on this and other local mines.

FELICITY—CENTER OF THE WORLD

(Although *National Geographic* has recognized Felicity and when scale permits, will designate it on maps, the townsite is not yet marked on commonly used road maps. It is located north from the I-8 Sidewinder Road off-ramp).

It isn't every day that we get to see a legend in the making, but such an event is this novel desert community designated by its creator as "the Center of the World."

American Girl Mine *in the Cargo Muchacho Mountains, 1969.–CP*

Now if this sounds a bit quirky, that's because it is. Jacques-Andre Istel, a former parachutist and investment banker, with his Chinese wife Felicia for whom the town is named, planted a time capsule under a 19-foot-high pyramid. In March 1985 they declared their townsite "the Center of the World." To quote the *National Geographic*, "On a spherical planet, one place has as good a claim as another to such a designation." Now incorporated, the town of Felicity also has been recognized as the "Center of the World" by the Imperial County Board of Supervisors.

Born in Paris, France, in 1929, Jacques has quite a history. His father was economic adviser to the French Premier Paul Reynaud when World War II began. Faced with the German invasion, the senior Istel joined General Charles de Gaulle's Free French forces and sent his family to America for greater safety. Jacques eventually became a naturalized citizen and after following a short career as a banker, became so fascinated with the art of parachute jumping that he joined the U.S. Marines. This endeavor granted him an opportunity to invent ways to make 'chutes more maneuverable. In 1961 he broke the world parachute record and left the Marines to found schools for parachuting. Today he is considered "father" of the sport.

One day in the 1960s, *Sports Illustrated* sent a young Chinese-American reporter named Felicia to interview him. Her father, also a banker, had moved his family from Shanghai to London when he was director of the Bank of China. It was there that Felicia was born. Later the family transferred to New York. So Felicia, like Jacques, had grown up in a banking family with international ties. By 1973 the pair were married and focused on "unusual" activities. They crisscrossed the Atlantic in a twin-engine Comanche plane five times. Later they made an even more daring flight across the mighty Pacific.

Eventually all this wanderlust took its toll. Jacques found himself yearning for clean air and quiet so pure one could hear a grain of sand grow. In the recess of his memory, such a place existed. He had passed through it as a second lieutenant in the Marines. Considering the nature of the beast, however, he knew that to settle without a challenge would be deadly. Felicia, endowed with an imagination equal to Jacques, accepted the idea. With no regrets, they set forth to settle this desolate parcel of land near the banks of the Colorado River. Financial help from his father, also a visionary, was forthcoming. Soon other interested relatives in France invested too. Jacques went to work to create his new city.

Felicity — Center of the World. The Honorable Jacques-Andres Istel, Mayor of Felicity and his wife Felicia, in front of their landmark pyramid.–CP

Meanwhile the imaginative entrepreneur was also involved in writing a children's book about a dragon called "Coe." One day Coe spoke out from a page of Jacques' manuscript to proclaim the town of Felicity as "The Center of the World." Not one to dispute a dragon, Jacques and Felicia proceeded to erect a pyramidal monument under which the official Center of the World would rest. "After all," reasoned Felicia, "any desert worth its sand should have a pyramid."

At present, the 2,700-acre townsite within sight of the freeway can boast of a restaurant, an attractive gift shop, a train station at which no train stops, and a few apartment houses. Future plans include a marble wall resembling the Vietnam War Memorial in Washington upon which individuals seeking immortality may have their names inscribed as a sort of index to personal "memories and messages" preserved for future generations in a giant computer on the premises. The future also includes house plots with "ample elbow room" designed to preserve desert views. Water is good, power comes from the Imperial Irrigation District, and buildings are attractive, but "quietude" still remains Felicity's most valuable asset.

WINTERHAVEN AND DRIFTWOOD CHARLIE'S LOST ARK

The site of the then non-existent town of Winterhaven felt the wrath of the mighty, untethered Colorado in the days when Yuma, across the river, provided a gateway to California. Following the abdication of Picacho's two ferries, a third entrepreneur entered the business. This one, L.J. F. Jaeger, established his ferry at a point several miles below the present site of Yuma, transporting the lumber to build it by pack train from San Diego. Until 1915 when the old highway bridge at Yuma was erected, Jaeger successfully carried countless gold seekers, pioneers and early desert explorers to California.

Then a funny thing happened on Winterhaven's way to achieving identity. After a legal boundary between the states of California and Arizona had been established by the course of the Colorado River, the river went astray and left a segment of populated land about 150 square miles in no-man's land. Authorities in California contended the land was theirs, as the boundary was set by the old river course, while Arizona asserted that when the river changed course, it automatically changed the state line. This made things rather hectic for the few hundred souls living within the disputed area. Both states wanted to collect taxes. Some residents voted in

Arizona; others in California. Still others voted twice. Until the matter was settled, residents were disenfranchised—American citizens, but technically residents of no state. Authorities in both Arizona and California agreed to assume no jurisdiction over the disputed area until the matter was resolved.

This, in time, began to please the inhabitants. Instead of being taxed by both states, they were taxed by none. Cars drove with no license plates. No laws were enforced. But when a man shot his neighbor and no charges were brought against the slayer because neither state had jurisdiction, the boundary dispute was resolved. In 1965 federal courts finally declared "no man's land" a part of Arizona. Law had come at last to this isolated pocket of the Old West.

The Winterhaven area attracts desert characters like a high powered magnet. Not only does it harbor the Center of the World, but until recent years it provided a gallery for a prominent folk artist known throughout desert lands as Driftwood Charlie.

When I first came across Charlie it was to do an interview for *Desert Magazine* when he was displaying his sculptures on the sands of Death Valley. They were imaginative, well-structured examples of primitive art. I was impressed. The shriveled gnome-like artist seemed as much a part of Death Valley as its crackled lake beds, so I was surprised some twenty years later to discover Driftwood Charlie's gallery moved to the remote, arid sands of the Quechan Indian Reservation located at Andrade, just south of Winterhaven on the Mexican border.

It was fitting that Charlie would remain in a desert setting. Once a boatswain's mate on a U.S. Navy gunboat that was sunk in

Colorado River, *a peaceful view somewhere near Winterhaven.–JRL*

Chinese waters by the Japanese during World War II, the former seaman had escaped countless dangers in every part of the globe. But when it came to retirement, he heeded the desert's call. "For the desert is much like the ocean," he explained, "with limitless horizons and dunes that roil like waves"—a comparison I had often made myself.

In youth, Charlie was apprenticed to an engraver, which explains why his creative urge manifested itself in sculpture. Only now instead of metal plates, he worked with media indigent to desert land, driftwood and stone. The sculptures exhibited in his gallery near Winterhaven differed from the earlier driftwood figures at Death Valley. Subjects there were dictated by contortions of the wood. His latter ones, carved from rock hauled from the stone quarry behind the Reservation's Sleepy Hollow RV Park, were inspired by ancient statues he remembered from his travels. Many are reminiscent of Easter Island and Aztec figures.

Charlie's work was praised in *Twentieth Century American Folk Art and Artists* by Julia Weissman and considered a treasure by collectors. Prior to his death in the late 1970s, he told visitors that his intention was to leave his work to the Quechan Indians, upon whose land he was living and displaying sculptures.

So what became of those weighty works of art? Were they carted away by vandals, or do some remain buried in sand on this bank of the Colorado River? Over a hundred existed when Charlie was interviewed shortly before his death by Brawley writer Peter Odens, to whom Charlie presented a huge sculptured head.

None of the Quechans, caretakers of the 44,000-acre reservation with its wealth of natural resources, has any knowledge of a legacy from Charlie. The tribal museum on Indian Hill in Winterhaven features historical artifacts, crafts and records pertaining to Yuman history. Perhaps Charlie's work would have been out of place there. Still, one would think that as a tourist attraction to enhance their river recreational projects some sculptures would be on display. But they aren't. So Driftwood Charlie's exotic work remains another treasure lost on the Colorado desert.

LOST MISSIONS—LA PURISIMA CONCEPTION AND SAN PEDRO Y SAN PABLO

Winterhaven's destiny has been entwined with Yuma's from the beginning. In the 1700s, two missions only twelve miles apart were established on the present California side—*Mision La Purisima Concepcion and Mision San Pedro y San Pablo de Bicuner*. They were built by four Franciscan padres from Mexico—Fathers Diaz, Morena, Garces, and Barrenecha—with a two-fold purpose. Firstly, to institute a way-station on the overland emigrant trail from Mexico to the California missions, and secondly to convert heathen Indians.

In this instance, the good padres followed a different plan than was customary. They established the two missions without a presidio nearby to provide protection. Unfortunately, the Yuma Indians turned out to be less docile than anticipated. They resented serf-like conditions imposed by the fathers as much as they did the assumption of their melons, beans, corn and scant pastureland by settlers and soldiers who passed through from Mexico.

The matter reached a bloody climax in 1781. Captain Don Fernando Rivera arrived with a large group of colonists and 1,000 head of cattle destined for the new city of Los Angeles. Believing that their grassland was to be taken by Rivera, hundreds of Yumans joined forces in a massacre that destroyed both river missions and cost the lives of Rivera, his soldiers, Father Garces and all other males at the mission. Women and children were made captive, later to be ransomed by Pedro Fages when he arrived in 1782 on his historic journey across desert and mountains to San Diego.

Historians of the past have puzzled over the exact location of the two Colorado River missions established in this area. No ruins exist of the wood buildings that were so small that they held no more than twenty worshippers. Not until Brawley journalist Peter Odens published an interview with the late Lee Emerson, historian of the Quechan Indians, was a definite site confirmed for the latter. Emerson's ancestors had led him to the site in his youth. At that time, there were still burned remnants of the church *in situ*. Due to Oden's investigation, a memorial plaque installed by E. Clampus Vitus, an organization dedicated to the preservation of California History, now marks the spot below an old cemetery about a mile south of Laguna Dam near the All American Canal.

As for *Purisima Concepcion*, some local members of the Yuman tribe believe that its foundations lies under the present St. Thomas Church beside the Yuman museum on Winterhaven's Indian Hill.

A legend told by folks in this area concerns some precious chalices buried by the Padres when they perceived growing unrest because promises made to the Quechans by the Spanish remained unfulfilled. Treasure hunters have made fruitless diggings all over the place. Failure may be due to the depth under which the chalices now lie, considering that the legendary burial spot is at the end of a dirt road leading up a steep incline to the bank of the All-American Canal. Most metal detectors will not register items buried below four feet.

STEAMBOATS ON THE COLORADO

By 1826, the hostility of Yumans necessitated a garrison to protect Mexican government mail carriers and Sonoran traders. This was the forerunner to the American Fort Yuma established in 1851. Today the fort is included in the Yuma Indian Reservation. The Bureau of Indian Affairs and an Indian school stand on the hill overlooking Winterhaven that once held the fort.

When the War Department needed an easier way to send supplies to Fort Yuma in the 1800s, it instituted a survey of the river below Yuma to determine if steamboats could operate up to the river from the Gulf. An iron steamboat fifty feet long and shipped in sections from San Francisco to the mouth of the Colorado was the affirmative result. Assembled in Yuma in 1857 and named *The Explorer*, it chugged recklessly up and down the stream, reaching as far north as Las Vegas Wash, for three-and-one-half months. It then came to an ignoble end with a stunning crash against a sunken rock. Like a ghoulish memory, though, its rusted ribs turned up seventy years later in the mud of a willow jungle on the Colorado Delta. Desert explorer and writer Randall Henderson identified the remains from historical sketches that had accompanied Lt. Ives' report of the early misadventure.

In spite of its short-lived run, the *Explorer* launched a colorful era on the Colorado. Other steamboats plied successfully between Yuma and the mines in Arizona and Nevada, reaching north to Fort Caldwell, now under the waters of Lake Mead. When the intercontinental railroad connected the East with the West, the day of the steamboats on the Colorado was brought to an end.

OLD PICACHO TOWN AND THE STATE RECREATION AREA

Entered from an offramp designated on I-8, the recreational area consists of eight miles of river frontage that extends some seven miles inland.

Picacho. *Gold was what first brought attention to this area whose beautiful, luminous landscape now attracts many recreational visitors.–CP*

On the northern fringe of Winterhaven where the river makes an eastward bend, are remnants of a route cut by mule teams that hauled gold out of Picacho and supplies from Yuma until 1908 when Laguna Dam prevented water transportation down the Colorado.

J. Smeaton Chase writes of a long lost village near the headgates of Laguna Dam named "Potholes" in reference to the wealth of gold nuggets that washed out of mountains above to be captured in rocky pots or pockets on the river.

To follow this trail to Picacho Recreational Area, cross the All-American Canal and proceed through verdant washes where palo verde sprawl like dancers in green leotards against cocoa-colored rock. These are the Chocolate Mountains, referred to as "purple hills" in Lt.Ives' 1858 Colorado Survey reports. Entering from this direction, the majestic part comes later and so suddenly that it leaves you totally awed. Don't be discouraged by the washboard road—rough, but easily maneuvered in a passenger car.

As the road approaches Picacho, extensive washes, jagged volcanic mountains, riverbottom sloughs and brakes surround turreted peaks so vividly painted with golds, corals, pinks and oranges that they appear luminous. Water is available at informal campgrounds and there are trails into primitive camping areas. In addition, the state park on the old town site has private camps, boat landings and fishing resorts.

Gold, rather than recreational diversions, first brought attention to this remote region. The original Spanish mine was discovered by an Indian in 1860, although Lt. Ives had seen evidence of placer mining here in 1858 when he chugged up the river in his little steamer, the *Explorer*. Nothing happened, however, until two years later when it was relocated by Mexican prospectors who developed it into one of the richest placers in California. At its peak, Picacho was a transported bit of Old Mexico. "*Oles*" cheered bullfighters in its arena, fandango dancers stamped to the clatter of castanets, lavish *bailes* introduced señoritas to romance.

Then enterprising Americans arrived to stake claims in the lofty mountain for which the district was named. The new breed of miner erected a large stamp mill near the river and connected it to the railroad. The place boomed. Picacho's payrolls amounted to $40,000 a month; its population grew to 2,500.

Celebrities from all over the world came to see the wonder of Picacho Peaks. Among them was Zane Grey, the famous writer of Western fiction, who found inspiration for his novel *Wanderer of the Wasteland* in which the hero described the peak as "towering to the sky, crowned in gold, aloof, unscalable, a massive rock sculptured by the ages." (Since Grey's day, the peak has been scaled.)

The total operations of the Picacho mills resulted in gold ore worth approximately $15 million. Ore from the mines was hauled to the mill by narrow-gauge railway. After milling, it was loaded on a steamer and taken to Yuma.

Long before bridging the Colorado River was considered possible, river ferries carried traffic into and out of the area. Two operated in 1849, transporting supplies and gold seekers across the river below its junction with the Gila on the Arizona side. The first was built to accommodate General Alexander Anderson and his troops. After its purpose was served, he presented a certificate of title to the Indians.

Then a second ferry was started by Lt. Cave J. Couts at Camp Calhoun on the California side. He later sold it to a descendent of Abraham Lincoln who had the misfortune to take in a blackguard as partner. The renegade, John Glanton, deftly did away with Lincoln and, at the same time, managed to destroy the Indian ferry in order to eliminate competition. He got his comeuppance, though. The indignant Indians in a surprise attack killed him, his men, and destroyed his boat.

Then followed more disaster! On a hot day in 1908 the over-loaded belts of the mine mill broke, exploding pieces of the giant flywheel through the roof to land as far as a quarter-mile down the slope. About that same time, the federal government further sealed the fate of Picacho by commencing construction on Laguna Dam, designed to curb the great river. No longer could steamers carry ore down the river. That, in conjunction with the mill accident and the drop in value of ore, ultimately brought about the final closing of the mines. Victimized by successive floods, the community fell to the mercy of thorny mesquite.

The mining town named for the peak now lies under the back-up waters of Imperial Dam along with a river road that used to meet the ferry. Today, old prospect holes, Indian sites, former Mexican "wetback" camps and fishermen's landings may be reached by the partially improved dirt trail through Indian Wash to Indian Pass and then down Gavilan Wash to the river, as described on the alternate route from Ogilby Road. What remains of the old townsite is now included in the state park.

OLD PLANK ROAD

With the advent of auto travel, drivers were stymied when it came to crossing the treacherous sand dunes until 1914 when the State of California decided to built a plank road. It consisted of two 2″ × 12″ wooden planks laid parallel to another plank and bound with cross ties. That one soon wore out, however, so two years later an improved wood roadway made of four-inch-thick planks attached to cross ties and bound with steel straps was constructed, with double sections in places to permit passing. Constructed in sections, when parts of it were temporarily inundated with sand they could be moved by a team of horses. The old plank road provided the only auto crossing in this area for ten years, until a highway was constructed. The plank road crossed the desert to the south, along a route now covered by I-8, where a freeway rest stop provides viewers with a small segment.

THE LOST PEARL SHIP OF JUAN ITURBE

As readers know by now, legends of ancient ships swept by tidal bores into the on-again off-again ancient seas that once filled this desert basin are legion. Relics of every kind of stranded craft from Viking ships to Spanish galleons have been seen or found from the beginning of desert history—some in Anza-Borrego Desert State Park's Fish Creek area, some on foothills of the Santa Rosa's west of the present Salton Sea, others adrift in sand dunes in this area.

Perhaps the legend with most historical credence concerns a pearling expedition from Acapulco composed of three ships under the joint command of Juan de Iturbe and Pedro Alverez de Rosales which set sail up the Gulf of California in March of 1615. After a brief landing at twenty-seven degrees latitude they were attacked by a force of hostile Indians, leaving one of their leaders seriously wounded. It was then decided that he should turn back to Acapulco while the other two continued up the gulf.

The black divers had been eminently successful in diving attempts, in addition to which Iturbe enjoyed great success in trading maggoty biscuits for pearls with friendly Indians along the way. Precisely what happened to Rosales at this point is vague, but possibly the two commanders decided that he should wait in a safe harbor with a fresh water spring while Iturbe explored further north. In spite of modern geological evidence that the gulf's extension this far north ended long before the Spanish came, an historical account reports that Iturbe continued north alone through a narrowing waterway that then opened into a vast sea extending far inland. Believing he at last had found the fabled Straits of Anian, so long sought by mariners to provide a passage between the two oceans, he reported that he had reached thirty-four degrees latitude before realizing his error. This is approximately the latitude of Palm Springs. (The present Gulf of California does not extend above thirty-two degrees, which is significant, although early readings were rarely accurate.)

Discouraged, Iturbe then turned south to rejoin the other members of his expedition, but found to his consternation that his ship was landlocked. Frantically he sailed around seeking an exit, to no avail. Further catastrophe occurred when he found himself grounded on a sandbar, with the sea abruptly receding, to leave his ship high and dry.

Forced to abandon the ship with its vast cargo of pearls, Iturbe and his crew somehow made their way on land back to the gulf shore. Subsequently they were rescued. Iturbe next turns up in history at Sinaloa on the Mexican mainland where he built a new ship and embarked upon a more profitable pearling expedition. Had early Imperial Valley settlers been cognizant of Iturbe's history and his valuable cargo, they might have more actively investigated reported sightings of a ship intermittently exposed in wind-blown sand dunes. But to them, it was just another victim of the "walking hills." So far as is known, Iturbe's immense cache of pearls still awaits discovery.

TRAVELS OF THE GOOD SHIP EXPLORER

Commissioned by the U.S. War Department in 1857, the *Explorer* was to determine whether or not the Colorado River was a navigable stream.

Built in Philadelphia, it was a 50-foot sternwheeler. After a short run on the Delaware River it was disassembled into eight sections, shipped by boat to the Isthmus of Panama, hauled over land to the Pacific, then by boat to San Francisco, and finally to the mud flats where the silt-laden discharge of the Colorado enters the Gulf of California. Here it was to be reassembled for the trip up the river—as far as it would go.

From the very beginning the sternwheeler and its crew, under the command of Lieutenant Joseph C. Ives, had problems. The hull was of cast and sheet-iron, with a 3-ton boiler mounted in the center of the deck. The idea was to stoke the boiler with firewood gathered along the shore as the boat traveled up stream. The men soon realized that the boiler was clumsy, oversize and warping the frame of the boat. To correct this weakness, four wooden scantlings were bolted to the bottom outside the hull. It was a makeshift affair that caused no end of trouble later in navigating the shallow water over countless shoals in the channel of the lower Colorado.

At the time of the Ives expedition, the winter flow of the Colorado was abnormally low, and the shallow water and frequent sandbars proved to be a constant source of struggle and delay. When the steamer would go aground the crew would jump out and push and tow until deeper water was found.

The Yumas who lived along the river as far north as the present town of Blythe would collect along the banks to watch the *Explorer* pass. Ives wrote in his log.... "their appearance is invariably the precursor of trouble. Whether their villages are near the places where the river is most easily forded, or whether they select for points of view where they know we will meet detention, we cannot tell; but the coincidence between their presence and a bad bar is so unfailing that Mr. Carroll considers it reason to slow down the engine when he sees them collecting on the bank."

The crew of the *Explorer* included 12 men. The engineer, physician and observer of natural history, a topographer, an astronomer-meteorologist and an artist and a naturalist. D.A. Robinson, a veteran river pilot on the Colorado and the proprietor of Robinson's Landing at the head of the Gulf, was recruited as captain and pilot.

Twenty-five soldiers from the garrison at Fort Yuma were supposed to serve as a military escort. Due to limited capacity of the boat the escort, with a pack-train carrying food and supplies, was to follow the old Indian trails upstream and stay in contact with the river party whenever possible.

The troopers weren't much of an escort because they didn't leave Fort Yuma until several days after the *Explorer* steamed up river. They didn't catch up with them until Ives was nearly 200 miles upstream on his return voyage!

While on its first voyage up the river the *Explorer* had a smashing crash when it collided with a submerged rock.

Ives wrote in his mariner's log, dated March 8, 1858. "For a second the impression was that the canyon had fallen in. The concussion was so violent that the men near the bow were thrown overboard; the doctor, Mr. Mollhausen, and myself having been seated in front of the upper deck, were precipitated head foremost into the bottom of the boat; the fireman pitching a log into the fire, went halfway in with it; the boiler was thrown out of place, the steam pipe doubled; the wheel-house was ripped away, and it was expected the boat would fill and sink instantly by all. Finding after a few moments had passed that she still floated, Captain Robinson had line taken into the skiff, and the steamer was towed alongside a gravelly spit a little below…"

After three and one-half months the *Explorer*, under Lieut. Ives, completed the arduous initial cruise up the Colorado with only the one serious mishap with the submerged rock.

The Secretary of War, John B. Floyd, on the basis of Lieut. Ives's report, declared the Colorado a navigable stream.

Without any further use for the *Explorer* it was sold to rivermen at Yuma who planned to use it for freighting between Yuma and Robinson's landing, where ocean-going ships deposited supplies for Yuma and other army garrisons in the southwest.

One day, after just a few trips of hauling wood, the steamer broke away from its mooring at Pilot Knob on the California side of the river opposite Yuma, floated downstream and simply disappeared from sight.

This ended only the first chapter in the saga of the good ship *Explorer*.

Seventy years passed. The men who piloted the *Explorer* and stoked mesquite wood in its huge boiler passed on into the pages of history. Yet there were those who read the graphic reports of the *Explorer* left by Lieut. Ives and they were mystified as to the final fate of the ship.

In 1929 rumors began to flow from the arrowweed jungle which covers the many acre delta of the Colorado. It was said that an old Cocopah Indian by the name of Calabasa had told of seeing the rusting hull of an old ship.

The Indian claimed it was partly buried in the silt in one of the many channels abandoned during the years of the Colorado's unstable wandering across the great delta.

Randall Henderson, publisher of the Daily Chronicle at Calexico, on the California-Mexican border, learned about the Indian's tale of an old iron boat and Henderson was sure from what he had read in Ives report that there was little doubt that this was the remains of the *Explorer*.

He envisioned it as an historical relic which would be put in Arizona's first state prison at Yuma, long abandoned and now being restored as a historical museum.

The search for the iron ship was a nightmare because, in the delta sector, only a crazy quilt of winding dusty ruts existed with no roads or bridges. Finally with the help of a local Mexican farmer in the delta's area they came upon the remains of the long lost *Explorer*!

Henderson's vision of a riverboat mounted within the walls of the old Arizona state prison "evaporated into thin air."

It was the *Explorer* alright but what remained was a sorry looking skeleton. Nothing but ribs left. Some of them still in place, but held together by such a fragile foundation of rusted iron and adobe earth as to make their removal impossible. "The sheet iron sides had all been removed soon after its excavation from its silt grave. The Mexicans in the vicinity had found a practical use for its sheets of iron. They made excellent griddles on which to cook tortillas" wrote Henderson.

And so it was that the old *Explorer* was still serving a useful purpose—and maybe that is better than being lost forever in the silt of the Colorado River bottom.

MINNIE SURLES

Educational Bulletin #92-2—A publication of the Desert Protective Council, Inc. (reprinted by permission)

POSTSCRIPT: MYTH OF THE DESERT

The first time I lay under the stars of the southern California desert, I slept little, listening through the night to the call of the wind as it roared through the land like the voice of the desert gods themselves. But although I was awed by the power in that voice, I was unable to translate its message. Choral Pepper's guide to the myths and mysteries of the desert has reminded me of that magical night. Now I understand that the desert gods were reminiscing, recounting their timeless tales of ancient seas, lost treasures, and vanished heroes. Their stories added a dimension of enchantment to the landscape around me and brightened every rock and lizard I saw.

Since the earliest families first huddled around a lonely campfire, stories have been shared and yarns spun. Some stories seek to explain the Big Mysteries, such as where we come from or where we are going. These are the stories we call myths: tales passed on through generations like collective dreams of the human soul. Other stories involve smaller mysteries (like where to find the lost treasures of Montezuma or of Pegleg Smith). But whether myth, legend, or lore, all good stories help us make it through the night: they entertain, they illuminate, they inspire.

"Once upon a time..." The words glow with promise. For a time, we will be entertained, amused, diverted, involved. Long before movies, long before television, before even books or magazines, stories offered what we all seek at the end of a demanding day: escape from our care-worn world into a magical land from which we return refreshed and renewed. Just as, for many modern men and women, the characters in a television series take on a life of their own, so the ghosts and spirits of a well-told tale live while the story holds our imagination. The need for entertainment, for escape, must be as ancient as the human voice, as ancient as the oldest stories still echoing through the desert dunes and caves.

But besides mere entertainment, there is another dimension to myth and story. By providing us with a glimpse into other worlds beyond the confining world of "reality" that surrounds us daily, stories carry us back to that enchanted place that we all inhabited once upon a time: a child's world, alive with wonder and mystery, a world where anything is possible.

The gray, harsh outlines of our lives become shimmering rainbows, multi-colored and surprising. Ordinary rocks on the desert floor become nuggets of placer gold; a flash of heat lightning is the dancing spirit of a beautiful woman haunting the desert hills. A good story, in short, allows us to experience the world as children do: with fresh spirits and open minds, with eyes to see, ears to hear and hearts to believe.

Finally, myths and stories illuminate not only the world around us, but the world within us as well. An empty cave in dry sandstone may, in the light of legend, prove to be the door to the center of creation; and that door to the center leads us back to ourselves. Throughout time and in all lands, the telling of tales has revealed not only the mysteries of the universe itself, but those of the human heart.

In *The Little Prince,* the author, Antoine de St. Exupery, describes a moonlit night in the desert thus: "I have always loved the desert. One sits down on a desert sand dune, sees nothing, and hears nothing. Yet through the silence something throbs, and gleams... When I was a little boy I lived in an old house and legend told us that a treasure was buried there. To be sure, no one had ever known how to find it; perhaps no one had even looked for it. But it cast an enchantment over that house...'Yes,' I said to the little prince. 'The house, the stars, the desert--what gives them their beauty is something that is invisible!' "

That is what the desert gods were trying to tell me that night so long ago. The myths and mysteries of the Southern California Desert are what give it its beauty, its enchantment. They describe "something that is invisible," the magic world just on the other side of reason. And they give beauty, not only to the desert around us, but also to all those dry and dusty places in our hearts. The stories are the true lost treasure of the desert, carried on the wind, hidden in the sand, recounted through the years for all those who can believe.

Judy Goldstein Botello is a pediatrician, lecturer and the author of *The Other Side: Journeys in Baja California; Adventures with Kids in San Diego;* and *More Adventures with Kids in San Diego.*

SELECTED BIBLIOGRAPHY

Ainsworth, E.M. *Beckoning Desert*. Englewood Cliffs, N.J.: Prentice-Hall, 1962.

Automobile Club of Southern California. *Southern California Desert Area*. Los Angeles, CA: Automobile Club of Southern California,1998.

Bailey, Philip A. *Golden Mirages*. Ramona, CA: Acoma Books, 1971.

Bieber, Ralph. *Exploring Southwestern Trails 1846-1854*. Vol. 7. Glendale, CA: Arthur Clark Co., 1938.

Caine, Ralph. *Historic Aztlan*. Los Angeles, CA: Self published, 1962.

Dawson, E. *Cacti of California*. Los Angeles, CA: University of California Press, 1982.

Drago, H.S. *Lost Bonanzas*. New York, NY: Dodd, Mead Co., 1966.

Gardner, Erle Stanley. *The Desert is Yours*. New York, NY: Wm. Morrow, 1963.

Geisinger, Iva. *Gold Rock*. Winterhaven, CA: Gold Rock Ranch, 1973.

Henderson, Randall. *On Desert Trails*. Los Angeles, CA: Westernlore Press, 1961.

Ives, Lieut. J.C. *Exploration of the Colorado River*. Washington, D.C.: U.S. Gov't. Printing Office, 1861.

Jaeger, Edmund. *The California Deserts*. Stanford, CA: Stanford University Press, 1965.

James, George Wharton. *The Colorado Desert*. 2 vols. Boston, MA: Little Brown, 1906.

Kennen, George. *The Salton Sea*. New York, NY: Macmillan Co., 1917.

Leadabrand, Russ. *Exploring California Byways*. Los Angeles, CA: Ward Ritchie Press, 1969.

___. *Mojave Desert of California*. Los Angeles, CA: Ward Ritchie Press, 1966.

Latham, J.H. *Famous Lost Mines of the Old West*. Amarillo, TX: True Treasure Publications, 1971.

Lee, E. Storrs. *Great California Desert*. New York, NY: G.B. Putnam, 1963.

Lindsay, Lowell, and Diana Lindsay. *Anza Borrego Desert Region*. 4th ed. Berkeley, CA: Wilderness Press, 1998.

Lindsay, Diana. *Our Historic Desert: The Story of the Anza-Borrego Desert*. San Diego, CA: Copley Press, 1973.

Mitchell, John D. *Lost Mines of the Great Southwest*. Glorietta, NM: Rio Grande Press, 1970.

Odens, Peter. *Dreamers, Adventurers and Storytellers of the West*. El Centro, CA: Self published, 1988.

——. *Picacho*. El Centro, CA: Self published, 1973.

——. *Along the Butterfield Trail*. El Centro,CA: Self published, 1982.

O'Neal, Lulu. *A Peculiar Piece of Desert*. Reprint, Morongo Valley, CA: Sagebrush Press, 1981.

Pepper, Choral. *Western Treasure Tales, Colorado*. Niwot, CO: University Press of Colorado, 1998.

——. *Treasure Legends of the West*. Salt Lake City, UT: Peregrine Smith Books, 1994.

——. *Baja California*. Los Angeles, CA: Ward Ritchie Press, 1973.

——. *Colorado Desert of California*. Los Angeles, CA: Ward Ritchie Press, 1973.

Pepper, Choral, and Brad Williams. *Lost Legends of the West*. New York, NY: Holt Rinehart, 1970 and Promontory Press, 1996

——. *The Mysterious West*. New York, NY: World Publications, 1968.

——. *Lost Treasures of the West*. New York, NY: Holt Rinehart, 1975 and Promontory Press, 1998.

Whipple, A.W. *The Whipple Report*. Los Angeles, CA: Westernlore Press, 1961; Amarillo, TX: Westernlore Press, 1971.

INDEX

INDEX

THE CALIFORNIA DESERT SERIES
from SUNBELT PUBLICATIONS
"Adventures in the Natural and Cultural History of the Californias"

Anza-Borrego A-Z: People, Places, and Things
> **By Diana Lindsay** A detailed guide to the place names and history, brought to life in 750 entries that chronicle the fascinating story of the region.

Anza-Borrego Desert Region 4th ed. Published by Wilderness Press
> **By Lowell and Diana Lindsay** Since 1978, the classic authority for the million acres of America's largest state park and the six adjacent federal wilderness areas.

California Desert Miracle: Fight for Desert Parks and Wilderness
> **By Frank Wheat** How under-funded volunteers fought to protect the last large area of wild land left in the state.

Campgrounds of San Diego County
> **By Jeff Tyler** The most current and detailed information available to one of the state's most popular camping areas including numerous sites in the desert.

Geology of Anza-Borrego: Edge of Creation
> **By Paul Remeika and Lowell Lindsay** An introduction to one of America's most active geologic areas, perched on the edge of the creation of new earth crust.

Geology of San Diego: Legacy of the Land
> **By Hal Clifford, Ted Bergen, and Steve Spear** A non-technical guide to the formation and topography of a diverse area of coast, mountains and desert.

Geology of Imperial and Mexicali Valleys: SDAG Guidebook 1998
> **Edited by Lowell Lindsay.** Five self-guiding field trips and related studies take the reader through this dynamic rift zone.

Paleontology and Geology of Anza-Borrego: SDAG Guidebook 1995
> **Edited by Paul Remeika and Ann Sturz.** Field trips and studies of the Carrizo and Borrego Badlands, and Split Mtn.

Palm Springs Oasis: Photographic Portfolio of the Coachella Valley
> **By Greg Lawson** An elegant full-color display of a magnificent desert and alpine region, which ranges from below sea level to over two-miles high.

Rise and Fall of San Diego: 150 Million Years of History
> **By Pat Abbott** Includes a self-guiding journey through Split Mtn., one of southern California's most spectacular chasms.

San Diego Mountain Bike Guide
> **By Daniel Greenstadt** Includes Los Coyotes, McCain Valley, Table Mountain, Valley of the Moon, Grapevine Canyon, and Oriflamme/Chariot Canyons.

ABOUT THE AUTHOR

Choral Pepper's name is closely linked with the literature and lore of the American Southwest. In addition to frequent special features for the Los Angeles Times and Christian Science Monitor, she was a syndicated travel columnist for twelve years, published continent-wide in fourteen metropolitan newspapers. Perhaps best known to desert enthusiasts as publisher of Desert Magazine during the decade of the 1960's, she has also written seventeen books including such southwestern classics as:

Guidebook to the Colorado Desert of California
Baja California: Vanished Missions, Lost Treasures, Strange Stories
The Mysterious West
Lost Legends of the West.
Treasure Legends of the West

In Choral's words, "perhaps because of a wanderlust nature, I gravitated naturally to writing travel. My parents started this trend when they took me to Europe at age eleven. Since then I have covered every part of the world. I've attended a mit-mit in Yap, dined with headhunters in Borneo, safaried in wartime Rhodesia while it was becoming Zimbabwe, explored Baja with the late mystery writer Erle Stanley Gardner, waltzed in Vienna, dined in Paris, shopped in Hong Kong, and had an apartment in London."

Join her now on a magical journey through time and beyond time in the Desert Lore of Southern California.